ACCLAIM FOR PERSONAL KANBAN

We're all constrained to just 1,440 minutes a day, so balancing work, family, and social responsibilities can be a challenge. The simple innovation of visualizing your work and limiting multitasking, explained in this engaging book, has me addicted and is paying off big time. It just feels more natural than other approaches and gives me a tool that I can use to manage my work and calendar instead of the other way around.

~ Michael A. Dalton
Author of *Simplifying Innovation*

Personal productivity systems usually fail in practice because of complexity—they don't reflect the collaborative nature of real work. Personal Kanban provides the simplest structure that could possibly work and lets you achieve a state of flow.

~ Ross Mayfield
CEO of SocialText

As an executive tasked with managing and creating innovation, my mind never gets to stop work at 5pm. In my experience professionally and at home, the methods described in *Personal Kanban* have greatly increased my productivity and personal satisfaction. I'd highly recommend this book to anyone who feels the need to make their lives more manageable and their use of time more effective.

~ Jabe Bloom
CTO of The Library Corporation

Personal Kanban shows you just how revolutionary the technique is. It's a must read for students to senior citizens who want to do fantastic work. Personal Kanban is simplistic and will become second nature; not only does it change with you and your life, it will change your life.

~ Patty Beidleman
Educator, Non-profit Organizer, Caregiver, Mom

Trying to get more effective? Why use Rube Goldberg systems of tabulated notebooks and special-purpose inserts? Instead, consider a system that flows like a stream and focuses your attention, both on the task at hand and on making your process more effective. That's what Personal Kanban is, and it may just fit your thinking and doing style.

~ Jerry Michalski
guide, Relationship Economy eXpedition

An important new addition to the transliteracy toolbox. And I'm enjoying the iPhone app!

~ Sue Thomas
Director of the Institute for Creative Technology
De Montfort University

Personal Kanban

Mapping Work | Navigating Life

Bob!

Great Timing! meet you @ Advice & Beyond! Live well work more

Modus Cooperandi Press

A Division of Modus Cooperandi, Inc.

1900 Nickerson Ave W. Suite 116-88

Seattle, WA 98119

Copyright 2011, Modus Cooperandi Inc.

Designed by Wayworks

Manufactured in the USA

ISBN 1453802266

EAN-13 9781453802267

PERSONAL KANBAN

Mapping Work | Navigating Life

by Jim Benson and Tonianne DeMaria Barry

FIRST MODUS COOPERANDI PRESS EDITION, JANUARY 2011

Cover Photo: © 2009 Tonianne DeMaria Barry

Taken At: Aldie Mill , Aldie, VA

Cover Design: Wayworks

Back cover cartoon by Jim Benson using ToonDoo: http://toondoo.com

Image on page 5, "Kanban Team at Work" used with permission by Kenji Hiranabe

Base image on page 49, "Trafficjam" used with permission by Lynac -

http://www.flickr.com/photos/lynac/321100379/

DEDICATION

Life is long. Life is short. We never do anything alone. Decades after they left this earth, the following people continue to inspire us. Their words and example at once fill our hearts and leave a void. It is to their memory we gratefully and lovingly dedicate this work.

For Jim:

Corey Sean Smith Who was the first person to truly help me realize my creative side. Who taught me that creative, intellectual, and spiritual expression were one and the same. Who was always more interested in doing than worrying. Who has never left my side.

Nellie Gray Hill Benson Who was around very briefly in my life, but has always been a model of what success really looks like. Driven, unassuming, uncompromising, flexible. You play the hand you are dealt.

For Tonianne:

Robert G. DeFelice Whose passion for the arts was rivaled only by his unbridled generosity and the enormity of his heart. My very own Uncle Drosselmeyer, he showed me from an early age you are never too old for fairy tales, magic truly exists, and angels most certainly walk among us.

Anthony A. DeMaria Whose passing was an incomprehensible loss, but whose faith in me is eternal. He was and remains my greatest teacher, and his words continue to inspire me. His fierce loyalty, insatiable thirst for knowledge, distinctly Neapolitan sense of humor, and appreciation for *la bella vita* are but a fraction of his bountiful legacy. It was a privilege to call him Daddy, and is a profound honor to be his namesake.

PERSONAL KANBAN IN FOUR FRAMES

Kan-ban is a Japanese word for "sign board."

PERSONAL KANBAN IS MORE THAN PRODUCTIVITY

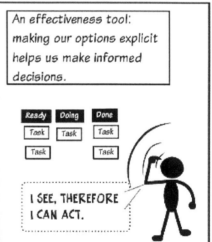

Personal Kanban provides context for our work, allowing us to
go beyond mere productivity and experience greater efficiency
and real effectiveness.

VISUALIZE YOUR WORK

TABLE OF CONTENTS

FOREWORD

INTRODUCTION

CHAPTER 1

CHAPTER 2

CHAPTER 3

My Time Management is in League with the Freeway   47

CHAPTER 4

Nature Flows   67

CHAPTER 5

CHAPTER 6

CHAPTER 7

ENDGAME

APPENDIX A

APPENDIX B

FOREWORD
THE AGONY OF
CRISIS MANAGEMENT

As an avid reader of business literature and a recovering human capital practitioner, most recently as Deputy, Human Resources at the Central Intelligence Agency, (retired), I've found *Personal Kanban: Mapping Work | Navigating Life* both insightful and timely. As we all cope in our own way with managing our work schedules and balancing our personal lives, others' expectations of us and our expectations of ourselves, we all suffer from work and information overload. While attempting to keep pace with the myriad knowledge flows, three dimensional conversations and constantly changing priorities among competing workflows, it is imperative that each of us forms new ways with which to adjudicate work; interact with our professional and personal colleagues—and our calendars—with due consideration for balancing what I like to call our "crap to fun" ratio.

Let's face it: technology precedes anthropology. The knowledge explosion, advent of social tools, new enterprise architectures, and complicated multifaceted workflows coupled with the exponential expansion of available knowledge and information is having a profound impact on how and when we do our work. This new knowledge environment is also impacting how we function both physically and mentally. The seemingly constant pressure to make hundreds and even thousands of decisions per day, some large and some small, and then act on those decisions is innately stress-inducing. Some have postulated that even our physiological brain development is being altered by virtue of how much time and focus we expend online, via mobile devices and constant access to information on demand.

Amidst this chaos and increasing pressure to function at a high level in a digital world where every keystroke is persistent and every thought expressed digitally impacts both our productivity and our personal brands, we are all personally challenged to keep our promises to others and ourselves, to balance work and family, the physical and the spiritual—while all around us our environments are evolving with increasing speed. Here, the gift to us all is resurrecting the tried and true concept of *kanban*, a "just in time" means of visualizing future, current, and past workflows that worked so well for the likes of Toyota (before their current challenges) and others—and then applying this framework personally as Personal Kanban.

Years ago while serving in a particularly demanding overseas position, I cut out an ad for an old software product (I don't even recall which one) that read: "Escape the agony of crisis management." I posted this on the whiteboard in my office, which I used both to communicate with my staff and, unwittingly, to categorize future work and work in progress against goals and objectives. In its day, that whiteboard served as an analog social network—as various employees came in to post updates and share information. It wasn't until reading this book that I realized how much better my personal productivity and health could be if I were to use that same approach in my personal and professional life. This work makes this methodology so clear and applicable to our personal lives, I now once again am using a whiteboard at my consulting practice using Personal Kanban as my roadmap.

The approach is both simple and elegant; clear and commonsensical. Without pretense or irrational demands, Personal Kanban offers several options for achieving better balance and peace of mind as we set about our daily tasks. From visualizing your workflow, understanding that your capacity is not the same as your throughput, to taking time to note your completed tasks (something at which I am very lacking, preferring instead to pummel myself immediately with the next task), I have learned multiple lessons from this book. It belongs on the bookshelves, Kindles and iPads of every student of healthy personal and professional productivity. It is the kind of work that deserves to be bookmarked, highlighted and referred to often as we all tackle our dynamic workloads, while constantly prioritizing and reprioritizing the next steps in our shared but personal journeys. Hopefully, you will find it equally useful, amidst all of today's distractions and high expectations, in escaping the agony of crisis management and balancing your own crap to fun ratios.

Tom McCluskey
Deputy, Human Resources (Retired)
Central Intelligence Agency
November 2010

Personal Kanban

Mapping Work | Navigating Life

INTRODUCTION
PERSONAL KANBAN: 100% NEW AGE FREE

I hesitated writing anything in this book that would smack of dimestore self-improvement or seem unnecessarily huggy and harmonically convergent. I wanted this to be a fun read—a practical one, to be sure—but certainly not one that promises the holy grail of time management. You'll find here no unwarranted claims of travel on the astral plane, or spiritual salvation through tracking your work. I am no self-help sufi or productivity pontiff. I simply want people to make conscious, informed decisions about the actions they take.

Professional life. Personal life. Social life. They are often treated as separate entities, but our lives and insights cannot be segregated. Work / life balance is a false dichotomy; compartmentalization is not sustainable. It forces life's professional, personal, and social elements to vie for attention, bringing with them seemingly competing expectations and goals. When we compartmentalize our lives, these elements become pathological, pushing us from one task to the next in an effort to satisfy their own jealous needs.

A leisurely weekend spent with loved ones, a perfectly manicured lawn, a winning business plan, an impromptu night on the town. Family time, work time, what we create, what we enjoy—it's all living. It's what makes you who you are, me who I am. Ideally we would find a balance between our daily routine, the obligations we feel compelled to satisfy (but don't excite us) and activities that rejuvenate us and feed our souls. This can prove challenging, because money is both a necessity and a major distraction.

For most of us, at least half our waking hours are spent at our place of employment. We measure work by measuring time: billable hours, punches of the clock, overtime. We assess our time at work by its monetary value: the hourly rate, the project bid, time-and-a-half. We approach and validate our work with an economic mindset: we work because we're paid. When we lack the tools to expand our relationship to work—our participation in it, our control of it—we become careless about what it is that we actually do. An economic view of our work becomes our *only* view of our work. When time becomes a function of income rather than personal or professional value, we become psychologically and emotionally detached from our actions.

If our goal is to live and work with meaning and purpose, this is not the approach we want to take.

As a supervisor and as an employee, I observed the impact of exchanging hours for dollars when time sheets were due. *What the heck did I do on Wednesday?* became a familiar lament. People were working so hard to complete work, they forgot what they had actually accomplished. There was no time to revel in accomplishments or even notice they had occurred.

We're all guilty of this, squandering our precious time merely trying to get by. We sequester joy for our evenings and weekends, scheduling time when we allow ourselves to live, rather than living all the time.

Fulfillment should not be considered an indulgence.

The following scenario is not uncommon: we go to work, we have little visibility into our co-workers' actions while at the same time, we offer them little transparency into our own. We are told to do work, but seldom understand why. We crave and deserve *context*. Without context, being told what to do is a communication failure. We cannot make informed decisions or create a quality product without first understanding *why* we are doing what we are doing. Lack of context creates waste, resulting in long work days, poor planning, and the inability to keep commitments outside the office.

Hoping to avoid these common mistakes, I turned to the world of productivity and time management. I soon discovered that while the tools had useful applications, implementation was often cumbersome and convoluted; the tools became chores. They took my time, energy, and focus. Some robbed me of my self-control. Even worse, most of these tools were solo flights, offering little opportunity for collaboration. Those sorts of tools didn't work for me. Tools should give you control and not take anything.

VISUALIZE YOUR WORK

I wanted to track and communicate my progress beyond the walls of my cubicle. I wanted to know where and when I could help my colleagues. I wanted collaboration and effectiveness for me and my team. I wanted a map of my work depicting not only the tasks at the office, but everything that mattered to me. Rather than being pushed by life, I wanted to pull life along with me.

I wanted Personal Kanban.

Personal Kanban is a simple, elegant mechanism that produces dramatic results. It helps us manage ourselves, but also lets us share our work, our goals, and our epiphanies with others. It's a visual launchpad to personal effectiveness, spontaneous collaboration, and an integrated life. It's low maintenance, but high yield. No crystals, no aromatherapy—just you, your work, and better planning.

CHAPTER 1
THE BASICS OF PERSONAL KANBAN

Resident of the 21st Century, consider:

> Your boss wants you to finish that report.
>
> Your accountant wants you to file your taxes.
>
> Your friends want you to show up for tee time.
>
> Your garden wants you to prune the hydrangea.
>
> Your daughter wants you to attend her recital.
>
> Your father wants you to call your mother. *It's been two weeks, you know.*
>
> Your bathroom wants you to re-caulk the tub.
>
> Your spouse wants you to just be present.

Confronted with endless obligations, you are overwhelmed. Faced with an onslaught of demands, you can't remember if you ate breakfast, much less deploy the mental reserves you need to survive the next two hours.

Is this as good as it gets?

Right now, all those things on your plate are just concepts. They are hard to prioritize, hard to analyze. You
need a way to actually *see* the tasks you're expected to
perform so you can do the right work at the right time,
and bring some clarity to the chaos. Personal Kanban is
a visual representation of work that makes the conceptual
tangible. It shows what needs to be done, what is complete, what is being delayed, and what is going on at this
precise moment.

There's a martial arts concept known as *Shu Ha Ri*, a
cycle of learning where first you learn the basics, then you
question them, and finally you find your own path. It's
not uncommon for someone coming to a book like this to
want to be told what to do and how to do it, without ever
understanding *why*. They want quick steps to easy living.
Life is not like that. It is variable. It changes whether we
plan for it or not. Our systems need to be flexible to adapt
to this variation. So, in this book we describe not only
the mechanics of Personal Kanban, but also the principles
behind it. We want you to understand the *why* and not
just *how to*. Afterwards, you can discover how Personal
Kanban practices fit into your life.

TOWARDS A MORE PERSONAL KANBAN

It's been well over a decade since I first began exploring ways to visualize workload to better manage myself and my teams. From 2000 to 2008, I co-owned a software development company called Gray Hill Solutions with my partner William Rowden. Gray Hill created collaborative software for government, usually in the area of Intelligent Transportation Systems. It was there that I first experimented with several visualization tools, including to-do lists, mind maps, and concept maps. To some extent, they all helped our teams see their work, but they weren't without their shortcomings. They would clutter quickly, fail to convey urgency, and become confusing when ad hoc teams collaborated on a particular item.

Of all the tools we explored at Gray Hill, floor-to-ceiling whiteboards covered in to-do lists proved to be the least effective. Rather than motivate us, we found them patronizing and demoralizing, revealing little more than the volume of work we faced. Thinking the medium might be at fault, we turned to databases, backlog management tools, even Microsoft Outlook to try to get lists to work for us, but the results were always the same: lists offered our work zero context, allowed for no reorganization or reprioritization, and obscured vital priorities beneath piles of marginally useful work.

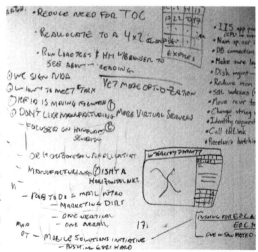

What we needed was a system that was dynamic, one that would help us prioritize and show us what we were currently working on. We then experimented with managing several large, concurrent projects using a shared mind-map. Using this visual control during our daily 15 minute stand-up, we were able to manage a shared backlog, pull tasks from that backlog, and limit our work-in-progress.[1]

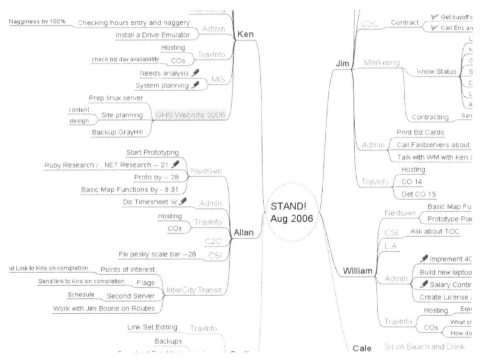

The mind map made Gray Hill staff positively giddy. It was the first time our geographically dispersed group had a constant and fairly comprehensive idea of what was going on. But while the mind map was a significant improvement over the to-do list, it was still lacking. It didn't help us complete tasks or distinguish between work

---

1   A daily stand-up is a brief meeting to get a status update on team members' actions. Perhaps the most important innovation from Agile methodologies, during these 5-15 minute meetings participants discuss what they've accomplished, current issues (blocked tasks, changes in context), and what is of highest priority for the day ahead. Based on their responses, tasks for the day are then assumed.

shared by multiple people. Its greatest limitation was that the information conveyed was not obvious. Text-based and small, with 8 point type on tiny branches, it offered us little ability to get a status-at-a-glance. As a project management tool it was useful, but it wasn't the information radiator we were seeking.

Fast forward to 2008. Corey Ladas, David Anderson, and I started Modus Cooperandi—a company built around collaborative management. At this point we'd all been using kanban-based management systems for software development: David and Corey at both Microsoft and Corbis, I at Gray Hill.[2] With kanban, we visualized the current work of our development crew on sticky notes as they traveled through a value stream—a graphic depiction of the steps in the software development process. The system was both simple and effective.

2   To read about Corey and David's respective personal journeys in Lean software development, see Corey Ladas, Scrumban: Essays on Kanban Systems for Lean Software Development (Seattle: Modus Cooperandi Press, 2008), and David J. Anderson, Kanban: Successful Evolutionary Change for Your Technology Business (Sequim: Blue Hole Press, 2010).

LIMIT YOUR WORK-IN-PROGRESS

Kanban for software development worked great for managing software creation, better than anything we'd used before. Its focus on team work increased productivity and effectiveness brilliantly. But we were overlooking a vital element—the individual team member. We still needed to understand how processes impacted our personal work.

It was at Modus that Corey and I put our heads together and created a *personal* kanban to visualize and manage our team's personal work. Our board was specifically designed to be an information radiator: we wanted it to show the flow of our work (even from a distance), limit our work-in-progress, and capture all tasks, not just those directly related to software production.

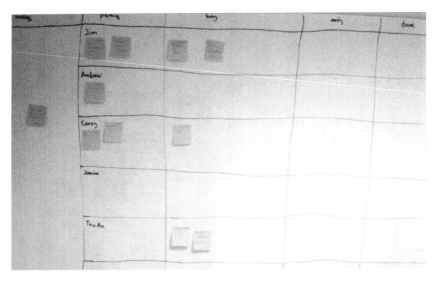

We paid close attention to the board's nuances. During our weekly retrospectives we discussed what was working, and what wasn't going as expected. We experimented with various formats, exploring ways in which this new tool worked best for the individual, and where it performed best for the team.

One thing was certain: in front of our board, we experienced our most intense focus, enthusiasm, and camaraderie. For the first time we could visualize our work—we could see its relationships and contexts—and we could interact with it. Beyond simply validating our productivity, our board fostered discussions that were expansive, enthusiastic, and revelatory. It stretched us far beyond our daily goals, taking us into exciting new realms of possibility.

We were operating under some basic assumptions taken from Lean manufacturing models.[3] We were visualizing work, limiting our work-in-progress, pushing decision-making to the last responsible moment, and continuously striving to improve. We learned that understanding our work is the key to controlling it.

In a manufacturing setting, organizational kanban visualizes how value is created, usually in the service of reducing waste and creating standard work. Adhering to this rule proved difficult in an office dominated by knowledge work. Knowledge work fights vigorously against standardization.[4]

It would take one more transition and several epiphanies to get beyond these issues.

In the middle of 2009, Corey went on a year-long sabbatical. Around the same time, I was offered a long-term opportunity in Washington D.C. Since David had left Modus to start his own company in late 2008, it made

LIMIT YOUR WORK-IN-PROGRESS

---

3   *There will be more on Lean and its relation to kanban and Personal Kanban later in the book.*
4   *Standard work consists of rigid processes to complete a task or create a product. Knowledge work is largely done in the brain, rather than by muscle, machines, or rote assembly.*

sense to close the office that after ten years and two businesses was packed with files, furniture, and work products.

Suddenly I was forced to deal with land management and insurance companies, telephone and internet service, selling office furniture, and finding temporary housing in D.C. The window to deal with these logistics was just a few short weeks and there were still client demands to be met. My personal life didn't take a break, either. I was moving across the country, and still had responsibilities to the two properties I owned in Washington State.

Even with the help of some very good friends, I found myself with more commitments than I could handle. The demands of multiple companies, clients, projects, and homes threatened to destroy my sanity. The overlapping nature of my work life, home life, and social life became clear. My need to quickly complete a disparate, overwhelming backlog produced a series of epiphanies:

> » Personal projects materialize out of nowhere.
> » Personal projects are often short-lived.
> » Personal projects can have their own unique visualizations.
> » Personal work is often unpredictable.
> » Personal work is difficult to manage.
> » The only way out is "through." Often, you can't delegate, procrastinate, or ignore personal work.
> » Context dictates the way we prioritize our personal work.

» Prioritization for personal work happens at the moment of doing.

» Other people's expectations of you do not disappear simply because you are overworked.

» Personal and professional life are not distinct and should not be artificially separated.

» Risk for individuals is inherently different from risk for a company.

I came to the realization that—like this photo—personal work is *messy*. "Organizational" kanban is used to seek predictability in work through visualization and refinement. While personal work can be calmed and tamed, it resists standardization. Therefore, "Personal" Kanban needed to be flexible enough to relate to an extremely variable or even chaotic workload.

I needed insight into how my work was being carried out, and how best to calm the stress. So I built that kanban—affectionately known as "Crapban." It was designed to deal with my laundry list of epiphanies, most important of which was that it needed to elegantly manage a highly variable workload and react to a dynamic work-in-process limit.

And it worked!

In a short span of time I burned through a substantial amount of work. When I was done, I knew exactly what I had accomplished, how long it took, what obstacles held me up and why. I was elated. My Personal Kanban showed me exactly what I'd done—*quite the opposite of not knowing what to put on your timesheet!*

Note: If you look closely at the left side of the Crapban grid, you'll notice I gave all those tasks initial prioritizations. Looking at what was accomplished, you can see that my initial prioritizations were quickly overcome by events. Premature prioritization was ultimately a waste of my time. Prioritization for personal work is highly contextual. Case in point, "Cancel L&I" was initially scheduled as task #14, but L&I called unexpectedly one morning and most of what I needed to accomplish with them was easily handled during that call. The context changed and so the priority changed.

Soon after I arrived in D.C., Tonianne DeMaria Barry and I continued to use, test, and blog about Personal Kanban. The approaches we wrote about were variations we used to get beyond my frenetic office closing and cross-country move, and begin doing business with our new clients.

It wasn't long before we began hearing from people around the globe who read the blog and tried Personal Kanban. Some were using it to organize their households, some to track student progress in their classrooms, some to manage a family member's treatment for a life-threatening illness.

Opportunities to use Personal Kanban professionally soon followed. Our engagement with the World Bank reinforced the flexibility of the Personal Kanban model. Planning to use it with a global team of scientists and researchers, we quickly discovered the Personal Kanban featured in most of our blog posts didn't fit with their unique needs. They needed to track more than simply work. Their context demanded that they track real-time issues, individual progress, and team progress every 20 minutes. We immediately created a new Personal Kanban visualization to display these elements and manage their particular workflow.

Personal Kanban has to be endlessly flexible. It needs to be a system that abhors rules. It's an enigma. A process that hates process.

How is this even possible?

RULES FOR A SYSTEM THAT ABHORS RULES

All too often companies respond to business needs by shopping for "proven" solutions, repeatable processes to achieve a desired outcome. They call these "best practices," which for many translates into *Don't tell me why something worked, tell me how they did it.* Rote, universal solutions exhibit little respect for the individuality of a problem, and epitomize lazy management. Their adoption often spawns professional organizations which certify legions of consultants selling one-size-fits-all processes. The end result is that good initial ideas become codified and ineffective industry dogma.

Imagine if I told you I had a simple, ten-minute technique—or worse yet, a twelve month program—guaranteed to fix any broken marriage simply because it was

toondoo.comcom-

built on marital best practices. How skeptical would you be? My guess (and my hope) is that your response would range between highly skeptical to downright disgusted. Instinctively, we understand that every relationship has its hardships and its happiness. On a personal level, we intuitively recognize that life is fraught with variation.

We appreciate and accept this variation when it comes to interpersonal relationships. So why not accept it in all aspects of life, including business?

Our lives are not static, and neither is our work. Personal Kanban evolves as our context changes, encouraging us to innovate and invent in response to the variation we encounter daily.

Our goal with Personal Kanban is to say *No* to those who presume to have our work all figured out. To say *No* to imposed processes that limit our ability to create false hopes of enforcing predictability.

LIMIT YOUR WORK-IN-PROGRESS

The Two Rules of Personal Kanban

Rule 1: Visualize Your Work.

It is challenging to understand what we can't see. We tend to focus on the obvious elements of our work (deadlines, individuals involved, the amount of effort needed) when the real context includes larger, unexpected, and more nebulous elements (passage of time, changes in the market, political impacts). Visualizing work gives us power over it. When we see work in its various contexts, real trade-offs become explicit. We now have a physical record of all those demands on our time. This larger view of our work and our context allows us to make better decisions. We can heartily embrace one task, while politely declining another.

Rule 2: Limit Your Work-in-Progress (WIP).

We cannot do more than we are capable of doing. This should seem obvious, but it's not. Our capacity for work is limited by a host of factors including the amount of time we have, the predictability of the task at hand, our level of experience with the task type, our energy level, and the amount of work we currently have in progress. Limiting WIP allows us the time to focus, work quickly, react calmly to change, and do a thoughtful job.

~

With Personal Kanban, principles take precedence over process. Process should change with context. Whether you choose to use a whiteboard or the back of a napkin, the underlying principles of visualizing your work and limiting your WIP remain constant, giving you the minimum structure to remain in control.

Think of Personal Kanban as a dynamic, interactive map that surveys your personal landscape for what excites, worries, or amuses you. It reveals what lies ahead (your goals, your upcoming tasks), where you are currently (what you are doing now), and where you've been (what you did, how you got here).

Like most maps, Personal Kanban depicts a wealth of information. It shows you:

- » What you want.
- » What you do.
- » How you do it.
- » Who you do it with.
- » What you complete.
- » What you leave unfinished.
- » How quickly you do things.
- » What causes your bottlenecks.
- » When and why you procrastinate.
- » When and why certain activities make you anxious.
- » What you can promise.
- » What you can say *No* to.

LIMIT YOUR WORK-IN-PROGRESS

Mapping our work allows us to navigate our life. It makes obvious not only the course we need to take to reach our destination, but also the terrain—revealing the amenities at our disposal and the roadblocks along the way. It plots our work's context (the people, the places, the conditions, the effort, the trade-offs), helping us to envision our real options. We begin to understand how we've made decisions in the past, and how we can make even better ones in the future. When we see the landscape of our work, we identify better courses of action because we have clarity.

WHY VISUALIZE YOUR WORK: NAVIGATE SAFELY

You get into your car to visit to your Grandma Tess. You adjust the seat and the mirrors, start the engine, and back out of the driveway. Navigating the streets of your hometown is deeply ingrained. You know where your grandmother's house is, you know the shortest route and the safest way to get there. Despite the fact that you've been making this trip for twenty years, you continue to rely on your vision of the road and the instruments in your car. You check your speed in the school zone. You make sure you have enough gas for the return trip home.

Your speedometer and gas gauge are "information radiators," passive yet indispensable objects that broadcast vital conditions such as the current state of your vehicle and the progress you've made thus far. Information radiators help us operate our vehicle safely and navigate our course effectively.

We don't dare drive without watching the road or checking our gauges, but oddly enough we manage our work blindly all the time. We don't visualize our tasks or rely on information radiators to alert us when our work might veer off track or require intervention. At best, we use deadlines to track our progress, even though deadlines are imposed, inflexible, and often don't respect our current context. Based on assumptions about the future, deadlines fail to take into account actual, real-time information.

We know our car gets approximately 400 miles per tankful. We know we last filled up around 250 miles ago. We know that city driving consumes more fuel than highway driving, and that missing an oil change can lower fuel efficiency. While we might be able to infer the level of our tank by our mileage, we would never buy a car without a fuel gauge. Without seeing the real-time impacts of our fuel consumption, it is likely we will run out of gas.

As automotive technology has become more advanced, we have more information radiators than ever before. As a society, we are becoming more demanding of our machinery. We expect real-time information from our cars, our phones, and even our kitchen appliances. We should demand no less from our work.

Personal Kanban is an information radiator for your work. With it, you understand the impacts and context of your work in real-time. This is where linear to-do lists fall short. Static and devoid of context, they remind us to do a certain number of tasks, but don't show us valuable real-time information necessary for effective decision making. It would be like covering your fuel gauge with a note telling you to *Buy gas when you need it.* The message is there, but the information is not. Personal Kanban gives us context, and shows us how that context impacts our ability to make decisions.

WHY LIMIT YOUR WIP

Cookie and the Cocoa Puffs

Growing up, I had a dog named Cookie. That's us over there. I'm reasonably sure this photograph was taken just a few weeks shy of this story, around 1978 or so.

Cookie didn't have the most discriminating taste, she ate everything. My family has countless stories, tales of leaving Cookie alone with objects three or four times her size. We would come back to find nary a trace of them, impossibly ingested by the unfazed poodle.

One night my brother Dave and I were watching *Logan's Run* on television, eating Cocoa Puffs from the box. Just two kids home alone having "dinner." Cookie, not surprisingly, wanted her share.

Who were we to deny her this most basic need?

When Cookie wanted something she would let you know. Her eyes would widen, she'd run around in circles, she'd make crazy noises. On that particular night, Cookie wouldn't rest and may have exploded without her critical fixx of Cocoa Puffs.

So I threw her one. And she caught it.

Then I tossed another one way up in the air. She tracked it, and swallowed it whole.

The third I threw directly at her, as hard as possible. *C'mon, it's a Cocoa Puff! You can't get a lot of velocity out of a Cocoa Puff!* She caught that one, too.

I followed up with two, then three. Cookie caught them all.

Finally, I grabbed a handful of Cocoa Puffs, and hurled them at her. Cookie panicked, her mouth hung open, her eyes tried to find to right ones to go for, her head waggled maddeningly and in the end…

…she caught nothing.

I can still see Cocoa Puffs bouncing off her nose and forehead. My brother and I thought this was hilarious.

Over and over we went through the progression. We tried four, five, six Cocoa Puffs. At four through six, she'd catch a few, but not all. In the end there was always the frightening deluge, handfuls thrown by my brother and me. Cookie nearly apoplectic, catching nothing. Dave and Jimmy laughing their heads off.

How does any of this relate to Personal Kanban?

Cookie had a provable Cocoa Puff WIP limit of three.

WHY CALL IT PERSONAL KANBAN

So why call it *Personal* Kanban if we can use it with our family, in the classroom, or with a team?

Personal Kanban tracks items of importance to the individual: tasks, appointments, small projects. They vary wildly in size, type, and urgency. For the purpose of this book, we'll shorthand these items by calling them "work."

Organizational kanban tracks items of value to the organization, usually creating something tangible like a widget, a report, a defined service. The goal is to understand the predictable and repeatable process of creating something, whether it's a nuclear submarine or a pastrami on rye. So organizational kanban focuses on standard work products, organizational efficiencies, and waste reduction. It takes a given repeatable process and replicates it, each time doing it faster, cheaper, and better.

People are less predictable than organizations. Individuals and small groups—particularly those involved in knowledge work—often engage in projects that are exploratory or inventive in nature. Standard work does not necessarily apply here. We want to understand the nature of our work, but not force it into some rigid process. Innovation relies on inspiration through exploration and experimentation.

Innovation requires improvement.

As mentioned earlier, Personal Kanban (and by extension this book) is based on the principles and techniques of a management concept known as "Lean." Lean is both a philosophy and a discipline which, at its core, increases access to information to ensure responsible decision making in the service of creating value. With increased access to information people feel more respected, teams are more motivated, and waste is reduced. Much of this waste reduction comes from Lean's goal of a "kaizen" culture. Kaizen is a state of continuous improvement where people naturally look for ways to improve poorly performing practices.

Personal Kanban facilitates kaizen. When we visualize our work, we adopt a kaizen mindset; we are weened from the comfort of complacency and actively seek out opportunities for improvement. Our brains become sensitized to patterns of waste and ineffectiveness. As we track patterns in our work, problems are made apparent and solutions become easier to find.

WHY THIS WORKS

On the surface, Personal Kanban is deceptively simple: visualize your work, limit your WIP, and pay attention to what's happening in your life. The psychology, neuropsychology, sociology, educational theory, and politics of Personal Kanban could certainly generate enough discussion for a series of books. This book is simply an introduction and more than enough information to get you started. So for now, let's just call attention to some of Personal Kanban's rudimentary psychological elements.

Comprehension

Neither our memory nor our to-do lists manage our work well. Tasks entangled in our mind or an assortment written down randomly robs us of clarity. When we're able to represent each of our tasks on individual sticky notes our workload assumes a physical shape. It becomes tangible. As sticky notes travel through our Personal Kanban, work becomes a comprehensible and natural system we can manage.

Kinesthetic Feedback 1: Learning

Before we learn to speak, we rely on our sense of touch to discover, interact with, and derive meaning from the world around us. Hands-on experience reinforces what we learn. Touching, feeling, physically interacting with our tasks transforms work-as-a-concept into work-as-a-concrete-experience. The physical experience of taking abstract ideas and turning them into tangible objects (sticky notes) impacts our learning by improving our understanding while promoting memory retention and skill synthesis.

Kinesthetic Feedback 2: Pattern Recognition

Each time we move a sticky note, we receive kinesthetic feedback: the tactile action is both a data point and a reward. A regular succession of these movements creates a cadence, a rhythm of work. Cadence creates an expectation. We begin to notice patterns (types of tasks most often delayed, tasks that require additional help), make distinctions (what work we enjoy, who we enjoy working with), and can adjust our prioritizations to suit.

Existential Overhead

Work we have yet to complete, or any aspect of our life that distracts us, creates existential overhead. As existential overhead mounts, our effectiveness diminishes. Visualizing work reduces the distractions of existential overhead by transforming fuzzy concepts into tangible objects that your brain can easily grasp and prioritize.

Narratives and Maps

Sticky notes flow through our Personal Kanban, converting work from static data into an instructional narrative. "The story" of our work is a familiar one, following the arc of stories from any era and any culture. Born in our backlog, work travels through different stages of our value stream where it develops, is tested, and ultimately finds resolution. While the arc of a story is simple to describe, the variety of characters, plot points, and elements of intrigue are as varied as life itself. Our work is our story, both interesting and instructive.

Personal Kanban defines and shapes our work in a way that lets our hand and brain interact. Physically and psychologically, it engages us in a framework for understanding not only what we're doing, but how we choose what to do, with whom we do it, how it gets done, and—when we're finished—the implications of the task we've just completed. This "story" unfolds on a map of our work which provides structure for the information. If you threw all your tasks on the floor, whether they were backlogged, in process, or completed, the elements of the story would exist but the structure would not. Personal Kanban provides a structure to make your evolving story coherent.

HOW TO USE THIS BOOK

This book is not your mom. It's not your boss. It's not your master.

Let me tell you why.

For several years I worked for David Evans and Associates (DEA), a consulting engineering firm based in Portland, Oregon. DEA assumed that you were a thinking, caring human being, and would manage yourself better than they could manage you. Their guiding principle "We find outstanding professionals, and we give them the freedom and support to do what they do best" taught me the difference between leadership and control.[5]

Good leaders provide enough management oversight to give a clear and coherent idea of vision and purpose, but not to the extent that they micromanage. They ensure employees have the information they need to make good decisions, and then step back to let the good decisions happen.

Personal Kanban (and this book) embody DEA's core philosophy. Neither are predicated on dictates or demands. Neither will wag a disapproving finger at you and admonish *You're doing it wrong!*

Personal Kanban (and this book) will, on the other hand, give you the freedom and support you need to do outstanding work.

LIMIT YOUR WORK-IN-PROGRESS

Remember, Personal Kanban has only two rules: *Visualize your work* and *Limit your work-in-progress*. Beyond that, you manage yourself according to your current context. You can create your own formats and value streams. You can prioritize in whatever way makes you most effective. You can conduct different kinds of retrospectives, depending on what's going on in your life at the moment. You can—and will—change your work strategies often.

So use this book as your guide, your springboard, your mentor. *Do not* let it become your bible, your drill sergeant, or your dictator.

It's *your* life. It's *your* work. It's *your* Personal Kanban.

Visualize your work.

Limit your work-in-progress.

PKFLOW TIPS

1. Personal Kanban is an information radiator for your work.
2. Existential overhead mounts when work is conceptual.
3. Visualization makes the conceptual tangible.
4. We can't do more work than we can handle.
5. Limiting WIP promotes completion and clarity.
6. Flexible systems adapt to changes in context.

CHAPTER 2

BUILDING YOUR FIRST PERSONAL KANBAN

Let's take a look at the Personal Kanban we've found fits most people's needs. This rudimentary format does everything we need in the beginning: it visualizes work, limits WIP, tracks workflow, and facilitates prioritization. This simple design is a launchpad. Use it to understand work and, over time, customize your approach to match your reality.

STEP ONE: GET YOUR STUFF READY

▶ **I've never drawn the same kanban twice. ~ Corey Ladas**

For your first Personal Kanban you can use a whiteboard, a chalk board, a bulletin board, a flip-chart, a piece of legal paper, the inside of a file folder, your office window, your refrigerator door, or a computer. Use anything that allows you to take the abstraction of "work I have to do" from inside of your head and put it in front of your eyes. There are no sanctioned steps, no official kits, and no certifications. You just have to be able to get your Personal

Kanban into a place where your work is accessible and obvious.

Having said that, I recommend starting out with a whiteboard, some dry-erase pens, and a pile of sticky notes.

Why?

A whiteboard provides just the right balance between permanence and flexibility. As your understanding of your work evolves, so too will your Personal Kanban. Your context will shift. Project types will change. Team members will come and go. You'll need to adapt your Personal Kanban to suit. You'll create new types of tasks. You'll add steps. You'll refine how you work. Simply erase and redraw as needed.

You may assume you already know your work, but you've probably never actually *seen* your work in action before. When we map out specific projects, almost instantly we begin to revise them. I've witnessed this with individuals, teams, and companies. They assume they understand their work. Some are even indignant *Of course I understand my work!* they protest. And their understanding is always almost correct.

Almost.

This seemingly minor disconnect causes all sorts of problems. It's difficult to plan for what you don't understand. I've seen team members at each other's throats simply because they all had a slightly different idea of how the team collectively created value. Since they couldn't agree on how their team worked, everything they did was based on a slightly different context. This meant there was always something slightly (or not so slightly) off with their planning.

Let's get rid of that disconnect. Let's understand how we work and how we make informed decisions. Just remember, Personal Kanban is an evolutionary system. Your context changes, your work changes. The more you use your Personal Kanban, the more you'll need to tailor it to the situation at hand.

So, your initial shopping list is:

- » A whiteboard
- » Pens (regular and dry-erase)
- » Sticky notes

VISUALIZE YOUR WORK

STEP TWO: ESTABLISH YOUR VALUE STREAM

▶ **Value Stream: The flow of work from beginning to completion.**

With Personal Kanban, you build a map of your work. The landscape depicted is your value stream. A value stream visually represents the flow of your work from its beginning through to its completion.

The most simple value stream is **READY** (work waiting to be processed), **DOING** (work-in-progress), and **DONE** (completed work).

Personal Kanban accommodates life's variation. Tasks change constantly, varying in size, urgency, ramifications, and "customer" (who you are doing the work for, which may include your boss, your spouse, your friends, or even yourself). With that much variation, it's difficult to understand the context of your work.

Personal Kanban helps you understand context. It helps you appreciate what you're doing and why. Need additional steps to complete a task? Not a problem. Personal Kanban's flexibility (and those dry erase pens) make it easy to modify your value stream.

STEP THREE: ESTABLISH YOUR BACKLOG

▶ **Backlog: Work you have yet to do.**

All that stuff we need to do? That's our backlog. Amorphous and undefined, our backlog is powerful and pernicious.

It's the ton of bricks on our chest that prevents us from breathing, the monster beneath our bed that stands between us and a restful night's sleep. It lurks behind every accomplishment, insisting *No time to celebrate, you've got so much more to do!*

The thing is, we tend to fear what we don't understand. If we don't understand something, we can't dispel it. If our backlog—the sum of our personal goals and expecta-tions—is unknown, and if as humans we tend to fear the unknown, then we risk fearing our own success.

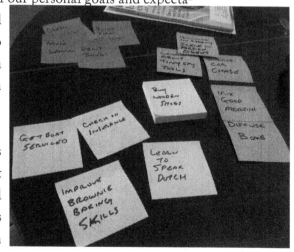

When our backlog is ambiguous—when it doesn't have a physical presence—our decisions are seldom grounded in reality. While we often allow our emotions to guide us, it's best to make informed decisions and for that, we need a clear view of our work.

Start populating your backlog by writing down everything you need to do on sticky notes. Everything. Big tasks, small tasks, get them all down on paper. Don't sweep things under the rug. Don't file them in a folder labeled *Tomorrow*. Don't lie to yourself. Wallpaper the room with sticky notes if you have to. You must confront your work beast before you can begin to tame it.

Later, you can record multiple tasks on a single sticky note, or batch work by color to make it more manageable. But for now, just concern yourself with getting tasks out of your head and onto those sticky notes. Your first backlog-fest should be an uncomfortable experience. You should at some point despair *There's way too much work!* But rest assured, overcoming denial, acknowledging the pain, and accepting it needs addressing are stages necessary in understanding our work.

When you are finished compiling your *initial* backlog (yes, you'll continue to add new tasks), lay out those sticky notes next to your board. If there are too many, well, then there are too many. Reality is harsh. Later we'll discuss ways to manage your backlog but for now, let's see it in all its glory.

Now decide which tasks need to be completed first and pull them into your **READY** column. You can set a limit on your **READY** column if you wish. Otherwise, you can populate it or configure it whatever way works best for you.

STEP FOUR: ESTABLISH YOUR WIP LIMIT

► **WIP [Work-in-Progress] Limit: The amount of work you can handle at any given time.**

No matter how motivated we may be, we're all guilty of leaving tasks half done or even mostly done, but not actually **DONE** done. Usually we're not even aware we've left them unfinished, because we've approached our work with little care, with lack of foresight. Without visualizing our work, we don't see the number of incomplete tasks we've amassed. This makes it nearly impossible to understand just how many incomplete tasks remain. Our brains hate this because our brains crave closure.

No really, they do!

Soviet psychologist Bluma Zeigarnik found that the human brain needs closure. This phenomenon—known as the "Zeigarnik Effect"—states that adults have a 90% chance of remembering interrupted and incomplete thoughts or actions over those that have been seen through to completion. With its tendency to seek out patterns to process meaning, the brain becomes preoccupied with missing pieces of information. Unfinished tasks vie for our attention, causing intrusive thoughts that ultimately impede productivity and increase the opportunity for error.

Tune in tomorrow – same Bat-time, same Bat-channel!

Do you set your DVR to record the latest installation of your favorite series? Do you stick around to find out what must-have gadget is being offered *Free!* when the infomercial pitchman advises *But wait, there's more?*

And when you don't, do you wonder what you've missed?

Our cognitive need for those bits of missing information causes us to ruminate over them. Whether it's unanswered questions relating to a TV character or commercial, or that unfinished home organization project we left mid-stream last summer, our inner voice nags us about how those half done or mostly done tasks aren't complete. The Zeigarnik Effect fosters a psychic tension which has a toxic interaction with fears or worries lying around in our psyche. What results is an anxiety feedback loop that can preclude sleep, impact health and for some, become psychologically or physically debilitating. This is that existential overhead we discussed earlier that causes us to be less effective. Visualizing work and limiting WIP neutralizes the cognitive overload brought on by the Zeigarnik Effect, dispelling uncertainty and promoting follow-through.

Personal Kanban provides kinesthetic, visual, and narrative feedback. When you pull that sticky note into DONE, it's brain candy. You're satisfying your brain's need for closure with three types of feedback. You know your work is done and you can focus on finishing the next task. Working like this is fulfilling. It bolsters self-esteem. Linearly finishing one task before embarking on the next commitment becomes addictive, a pattern, and eventually a habit.

So what's the easiest and most effective way around these tasks? Go through them. Get them off your plate. Get the work done.

But how? There's so much to do!

Our first phase in this battle of the obliged is to limit the number of things we do at any given time. This is our work-in-progress, our WIP.

Flameau The Juggler: A Study in WIP

It's the last weekend of the summer. Flameau, a regular fixture on the boardwalk, barely unpacks his props before a crowd begins to form. His reputation precedes him, and even before his assistant Flamette lights the first torch, eager onlookers begin to throw money into his tip hat, waiting to be dazzled by the pyro-juggler's promise of tonight's "unprecedented finale."

Flameau removes his cape and with a steady gaze begins his show. Carefully he catches each torch Flamette tosses. One, two, three flaming torches, Flameau calmly juggles away. Two torches are simple. Three are second nature. His timing is perfect. His coordination is flawless. His audience is rapt.

Soon Flameau has four, then five torches mid-juggle. His performance begins to show just the slightest signs of stress, but dozens of enthralled onlookers hardly notice. Dazzled by the sight before them and the promise of what's ahead, their suspense continues to build.

It isn't long before Flameau has six, then seven torches under his control. The furrows forming on his brow begin to belie the performers confidence. As his mental pressure rises, fears which usually lie buried in his psyche begin to surface.

What if Flamette wants me to fail?

Maybe there's a reason Lisa didn't send me her usual good morning text. His mind strays to thoughts of his girlfriend.

What if I don't get into that MBA program, and I'm stuck on this boardwalk for the rest of my life? He ruminates over his future.

He's now juggling eight torches. Movements that were once fluid are now jerky, even panicked. Anxious, agitated, it's patently obvious Flameau is becoming unglued.

Then, within seconds of catching that ninth and final torch, Flameau misses a handoff and sets himself on fire. Torches fly into the crowd like arrows blazing. The crowd scatters, screaming. Flameau's juggling career is in cinders.

Flameau's Aftermath: The Importance of Limiting WIP

So what does Flameau teach us? A few torches may be easy to juggle, but that doesn't give Flameau infinite capacity for *just one more.* Nor does it suggest that juggling just under his breaking point is a good idea, either. As we witnessed with

Cookie, the closer you get to reaching your capacity, the more stress taxes your brain's resources, and impacts your performance. As Flameau's active torches moved from three (comfortable) to four then five (less comfortable) to six and seven (unnerving) to eight (breaking point), stress reaches into the recesses of his mind and pulls out painful memories and—combined with his insecurities and fears—converts them into WIP. Moments of heightened stress can translate into more WIP than we realize, because we're simultaneously battling our fears in addition to doing more work. Whether it involves catching Cocoa Puffs or flaming torches, increasing work linearly increases the likelihood of failure exponentially.

Even jugglers can only control so many things at once. The more work we take on the less steady we remain and the more stressed we become. Research consistently shows we cannot reach our maximum effectiveness while multitasking. Instead, maximum effectiveness results when we limit our WIP and focus on the task before us.

Flameau's insecurities with his girlfriend Lisa were not new. They were always there, lying dormant, waiting to surface with the first sign of stress. These doubts were existential overhead kept in check so long as his brain had ample capacity to process those worries quietly in the background. But as he overextended himself, his brain could no longer shuffle off that overhead into an empty corner, there were simply no corners left.

Personal Kanban helps us find the sweet spot, that point where we do the optimal amount of work at the optimal speed; where our work is manageable and enjoys the slack necessary to deal with other areas of life. For both Cookie and Flameau, the sweet spot was three.

To find your work's sweet spot, start by setting an arbitrary WIP limit, let's say no more than three tasks. Add this number to your **DOING** column. Just be sure to begin with a number that is realistic and comfortable, and expect that number to change. On days when you are motivated and energized, your WIP capacity will increase. Conversely, if there is an emergency that requires your attention, your WIP limit should decrease. Understanding our capacity allows us to rise to challenges no matter our current context. Our Personal Kanban reflects how we react in all situations, and shows us what we need to be effective.

STEP FIVE: BEGIN TO PULL

▶ **Pull: To bring a task into DOING when you have capacity for it.**

So you've built your Personal Kanban. You have a value stream, a backlog, and a WIP limit.

Now it's time to pull.

Each time you pull a task from **READY** into **DOING**, you're prioritizing based on your current context. As you work, look for ways to pull more effectively. Ask yourself questions like *Which is the most pressing task? Which tasks can I fit into this half hour before I leave for my meeting? Which tasks can I batch together?*

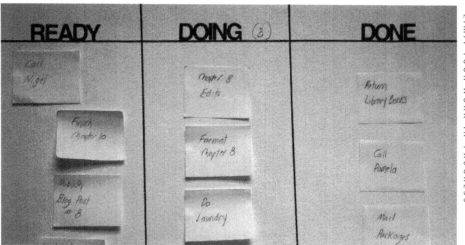

LIMIT YOUR WORK-IN-PROGRESS

With these questions in mind, reach into your **BACKLOG** and pull a few tasks into **READY**. Then, based on your context, pull the highest priority tasks into **DOING**. Pull no more than your WIP limit. As you complete a task, pull it into **DONE**.

Pulling tasks is simple yet vital. The physical act of moving sticky notes across a value stream to change their status satisfies our brain's need for closure. It's a kinesthetic expression of completion, an antidote for the Zeigarnik Effect.

Personal Kanban is a pull-based system. We pull work into **DOING** only when we have room to accommodate it. Pulling is a willful act. This is different from "pushing," which is how we normally take on work. In a push system, people tell you what to do and when to do it, regardless of whether you have capacity for it or if it is really the highest priority task at the time.

STEP SIX: REFLECT

After a few days, your **DONE** column should be getting pretty full, that's proof you've been productive. But Personal Kanban doesn't stop there. Now it's time to find out if you've been effective. Take a moment to consider the following:

> » Which tasks did you do particularly well?
> » Which tasks made you feel good about yourself?
> » Which tasks were difficult to complete?
> » Were the right tasks completed at the right time?
> » Did the tasks completed provide value?

Then ask yourself *Why?*

Congratulations! You just completed your first "retrospective," a processing loop that lets you give thought to what you're doing, why and how you're doing it, what you do best, and where there's room for improvement.

PERSONAL KANBAN POWER BOOSTERS

The following optional techniques will make your Personal Kanban work a little harder.

Individuals as well as teams have unique ways of working. When you begin a project large enough to require its own dedicated Personal Kanban, first ask yourself *How does this project really flow?*

Consider this scenario: you're part of a committee writing a grant application. You've organized a team, and each member is responsible for writing one section. Once the individual sections are written, the group edits them and finalizes the document. The value stream for the grant application might look like:

BACKLOG » WRITING » IN REVIEW » REVISION » FINAL REVIEW » FINAL DRAFT » COMPLETE

Even with small projects, watch for predictable stages in work and make sure your Personal Kanban takes them into account. Every time your work involves another person or something happens outside your immediate control, make sure it is reflected on your board.

Why?

These are the stages where delay and waste can be injected into your process. When work flows to a point and stagnates, this is known as a "bottleneck," a constraint that prevents work from flowing. You want to be able to visualize these points. As you watch work flow through your value stream, you'll see where work moves smoothly, where work is slowing down, or where work comes to a standstill.

Two Basic Personal Kanban Options

At Modus Cooperandi, our Personal Kanban has two simple columns to help organize and prioritize our work. Later, we discuss prioritization (different ways to choose the right work at the right time) and design patterns (different ways to visualize work) in depth. As we just saw with the workflow for writing a grant application, value streams can become complex. But we can work up to complex.

For now, let's just explore adding two additional columns to our basic **READY -> DOING -> DONE** value stream. Again, these are optional. Implement them if you like, but only if you feel they'll suit your context.

The Pen

Ideally, we choose a task, see it through to completion, and then pull the next. Realistically, personal work isn't so clear-cut. We can't always be autonomous. We rely on others for input, things to be delivered, or the passage of time for our tasks to be completed.

Sequester tasks that are not yet complete but you can't move forward on in a column called **THE PEN**. These tasks await additional action that is often beyond your control. For example, say one of your tasks is "Schedule Painters." You take that task from **READY**, pull it into **DOING** and call the painters. It's 6:30 PM after their normal business hours and so you leave voice mail.

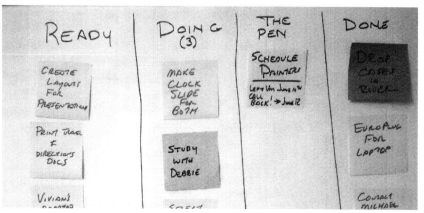

If you have a WIP limit of three and you leave three voice mail messages, suddenly you can't work. You've met your WIP limit.

You want to make sure that the tasks you place in **THE PEN** are awaiting additional input. If you're stuck on a task that doesn't require external assistance, resist the temptation to put it in this column. It's best to just work through it. If it is truly blocking you, call a friend or a colleague to help. Otherwise, you'll load up **THE PEN** with every task that causes you angst.

While you're temporarily sequestering tasks in **THE PEN**, keep in mind that clarity is still the goal. You'll want to add a prompt such as *Left voice mail on June 10th. Make follow-up call on June 12th.* That way, a task slips out of your WIP, but not without ensuring you have a reminder to revisit the task before it goes stale. Always be sure items in **THE PEN** are actionable.

To ensure **THE PEN** doesn't become a glorified junk lane, assign it a WIP limit. You should never find your **BACKLOG** empty while **THE PEN** is filled with half done tasks. Always refer to **THE PEN** first when pulling tasks into **DOING**.

Tasks can lose relevance and so, like any other type of pen, it may need to be cleaned every so often. Don't let **THE PEN** become a visual representation of your procrastination.

Today

The **TODAY** column is where you pull tasks you expect to accomplish, you guessed it, *today*. Our circadian rhythms are firmly rooted in our psyche. This is that 24-hour internal clock that tells us whether we should be waking or sleeping or wondering when dinner will be ready.

Physiologically and psychologically we are attuned to the concept of a day. It's our primary reference point, it's what we measure our success against. Whether we show up at the office at 7:30 Monday morning or wake up at noon Saturday during our holiday in Maui, we automatically think *Today I'm going to...* and mentally list our goals for

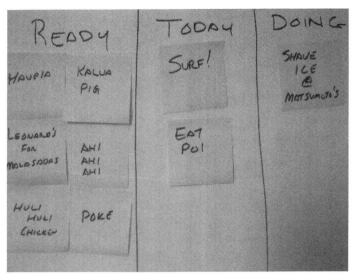

the day. Remember, relaxing is a legitimate and justi-fiable goal. If you're planning to surf and eat poi, then those goals should appear in your **TODAY** column.

The thing is, we rarely get to tackle—let alone com-plete—everything we set out to do. So at the end of the day our mental **TODAY** column is populated with tasks we wanted to have accomplished. We end up preoccu-pied with our incomplete tasks (remember the Zeigarnik Effect), while devaluing our actual accomplishments. Sure, we may have accomplished some awesome work, but we fail to recognize it because we didn't accomplish *everything* we intended to do. Well, everything was prob-ably an unreasonable goal in the first place.

The **TODAY** column shows us the difference between what we want to do each day and what we can actually achieve. It shows us how we fall short of our daily goal. Once we understand our actual daily capability, we can set more realistic goals at the beginning of the day, and end the day feeling we've been effective.

WHAT IT ALL MEANS

Chapter 2 is the how of Personal Kanban. This stand-alone chapter gives you all the basic information you need to get started. In the pages that follow, you can learn why these steps work and how to extend them.

PKFLOW TIPS

1. Let your context be your guide—change your Personal Kanban as needed.

2. Be honest about your backlog.

3. Your value stream may be adapted for specific projects.

4. Visualizing the nature of your work is the key to seeing what is really happening.

5. When WIP limits are exceeded, stress results.

6. Expect the unexpected.

CHAPTER 3
MY TIME MANAGEMENT IS IN LEAGUE WITH THE FREEWAY

▶ **Well it just goes to show you, it's always something. You either got a toenail in your hamburger or toilet paper clinging to your shoe.**
~ Roseanne Roseannadanna

FLOW LIKE TRAFFIC

Capacity: How much stuff will fit

Throughput: How much stuff will flow

They are not synonymous.

All too often we equate "free time" with "capacity." We assume that if we don't have an activity scheduled, we can fit in more work. The calendar shows a free hour, so we must have time for another meeting or another phone call or another trip to the post office, right?

Wrong.

This is why people who gauge their "free" time by the whitespace on their calendar usually run behind schedule. They rarely allow for slack between one appointment and the next, and any interruption in their schedule cascades through to the end of the day.

More Water Sir?

When the waiter comes by to replenish our half empty water glass, we expect it to be topped off. Room in the glass means more room for water. We liken ourselves to that glass, assuming if the glass can handle more water until it's full, we too can handle more work until we're full. But we're actually not like that glass at all. For us, "full" doesn't refer to our capacity, it refers to our throughput. We don't contain work, we process it.

We are actually more in league with the freeway.

Like that glass, a freeway ranges between 0 and 100% capacity; it can be anywhere from totally empty to completely filled with vehicles. But unlike that glass, the freeway doesn't optimize for capacity, it optimizes for throughput. Capacity is a spatial relationship, while throughput is a flow relationship.

Some of us are cautious drivers, while others are aggressive. The roadway has to accommodate all driving styles. This means that at a certain level of congestion, traffic begins to slow; it reaches its maximum throughput.[1] The more vehicles, the greater the variation in driving styles, the slower traffic becomes, and the more its flow becomes

---

1   As an urban planner, my rule of thumb was 65% capacity as the point where congestion became likely.

constrained. Traffic can only move as fast as the slowest vehicles on the road. We begin to experience congestion, even though the roadway may only be at 65% capacity.

As the freeway approaches 100% capacity, it ceases being a freeway. It becomes a parking lot.

Capacity is an ineffective measure of throughput, and a horrible way to gauge what we can do. It doesn't measure how we actually work, or at what rate we actually work.

Capacity is merely a brute force measure of what will fit.

Like traffic, work does not fit. Work flows.

When we don't acknowledge or respect our work's flow, we fall prey to multitasking. After a while we lose touch with a task here, a task there. We rush through one thing to get to the next, striving for quantity (productivity) when we know quality (effectiveness) will surely suffer. In the end, we achieve neither.

That motorcyclist in the picture is that last little five minute task you agreed to do.

It's just five minutes! How could I possibly say no?

A 2009 Stanford University study dispels the myth that multitaskers have a mental edge over those who focus on a single task, ultimately deeming multitasking counterproductive.[2] On a wide battery of tests, participants who identified as high multitaskers performed uniformly worse than their counterparts who claimed to be low multitaskers. This included tests that one might assume high multitaskers would perform well on, such as following directions with multiple stimuli or rapidly switching from one task to another.

High multitaskers optimize for capacity and not for throughput. They were unable to effectively manage multiple streams of information simultaneously. When asked to ignore one data set and concentrate on another, they had trouble filtering the data. They simply took in everything, overtaxing their ability to focus and complete assignments. Low multitaskers proved better able to filter their environment and process appropriate information.

When we multitask, our brain tries to process several streams of information concurrently. It does this by literally "splitting the brain," dividing the work between its two hemispheres, with each half of the brain corresponding with and focusing on a specific task.[3] With only two hemispheres to process related mental activities, three or more activities overstimulate the brain, resulting in mental congestion. We become easily distracted and struggle to accomplish even the simplest tasks. In essence, the brain's highway is filling with work. After a while it starts

---

2 . http://news.stanford.edu/news/2009/august24/multitask-research-study-082409.html

3 http://news.sciencemag.org/sciencenow/2010/04/multitasking-splits-the-brain.html

to slow down, eventually arriving at gridlock or mental burnout.

We don't want our roadways or our work gridlocked, we want *flow*. We want *throughput*. Throughput is a flow-based system. It measures success by the amount of quality work flowing from **READY** to **DONE** over time, not just the volume of work we can cram into our schedule.

Personal Kanban gives us insight into how our work flows—where flow is optimal, where flow is blocked. The rate at which work moves from **READY** to **DONE** is our throughput—our real throughput, not our guess at it. Throughput is something we can measure, appreciate, and use to make informed decisions. We can begin to manage our work by our ability to thoughtfully complete tasks.

Reality Check

There will be days when interruptions and dynamic prioritizations will be the norm. While multitasking is certainly not ideal, having the flexibility to multitask when the situation calls for it is. Context should always inform your actions. Sometimes your Personal Kanban will have to accommodate the demands of a busy day. When that happens, look for ways to reduce the flow of unexpected work.

SETTING WIP LIMITS

Let's return to Cookie and the Cocoa Puffs. After exceeding her WIP limit, Cookie not only began to miss Cocoa Puffs, but the experience became traumatic. A glutton for punishment, she returned again and again for another stressful encounter.

Realistically speaking, there's a little Cookie in each of us.

And life? It's that twisted 13 year-old kid bombarding us with handfuls of breakfast cereal, throwing tasks at us at a bewildering rate. Not only can't we catch them, they scare the hell out of us. Yet we come back for more, overloading our workload, adding that one extra task.

We need to control our workload. We need to divide it into manageable chunks and finish what we start. We need a WIP limit.

Initially, your WIP limit will be an arbitrary number, perhaps two or three. That's just a starting point, and merely a suggestion. See what works for you. The goal here is to start limiting what you're doing and take care to finish what you begin.

With time, you'll notice the situation at hand—your context—will dictate your WIP limit. If tasks tend to languish, try reducing your WIP limit. If you find you're constantly pulling sticky notes into **DOING**, you might be able to handle more work. Either increase your WIP limit or consider tracking more broadly-defined tasks.

While this might be a simplistic way of looking at WIP, right now we're just easing into it. Articles on personal-kanban.com delve deeper into WIP: what it means, how it's measured, and what its impacts are. In the beginning, it's advisable to focus on the flow of your work and the idea that your work actually has a "shape." So go ahead, experiment with your WIP limit. Just don't become obsessive about it.

LIVING THE DAYS OF OUR LIVES

Do we want to let our days slip by,
like sands through the hourglass?

Or do we want to live them purposefully,
like chapters in a novel?

When I supervised a large staff, they were responsible for filling out their time sheets. Admittedly, this task is hardly one to get excited over, and so the pushback I received was understandable. For the longest time, I attributed their resistance to the task's tedium. But there were other tedious tasks (like changing the printer toner) that people did without reservation. It wasn't mere apathy, so what could it be?

It was the Zeigarnik Effect! Preoccupied with their unfinished tasks, work they actually completed became a blur. Imagine, forgetting your accomplishments!

And forget they did. Ubiquitous head-scratching and cries of *What the hell did I do this week?* would launch crazy forensic research projects to recreate the activities of the days in question. They'd look for clues in anything with a time or date stamp—calendars, email, faxes, mobile phone history—in their quest for answers about just what happened during the course of the week.

Time lost searching for lost time.

Frankly, that's terrifying. Hours, days, weeks of our lives vanish into the ether. Precious time we'll never recoup because we aren't paying attention to what we're doing, *we're just endlessly and mindlessly doing*. By visualizing your backlog, your WIP, and your completed tasks, Personal Kanban rewards you for recording the good work you've done and knowing what comes next.

If you can't remember it, you can't improve it.

With Personal Kanban, you can begin to critically assess your actual work. You can compare past actions and future opportunities to discover the most effective and the most meaningful. You can make decisions that are aligned with—and balance out—your immediate needs and your long-term goals. You can decide whether your energy at any given moment is best directed toward achieving a professional certification, playing Scrabble with your kids, or painting your living room.

Sometimes our priorities appear unrelated. It's doubtful that your long-term investment goals are contingent on scrubbing your kitchen counters, but those goals will certainly be impacted should you poison yourself in a kitchen filled with *E. coli* and have to go on disability. You want to weigh your options based on a multitude of variables. Options have unexpected relationships, and so your decisions should be based on your entire portfolio of need. In management terms, this is known as "risk assessment."

LIMIT YOUR WORK-IN-PROGRESS

Personal Kanban helps you assess the risks and rewards of specific tasks by showing you:

» What is your true investment of time and energy.

» What pitfalls may accompany a particular task.

» Whether certain tasks are usually predictable or unpredictable.

» Which tasks involve people you like.

» Which tasks you enjoy or excel at.

With insight into the costs and values of specific types of work, Personal Kanban helps you make decisions based on a deeper understanding of your work's context.

We write down, track, and archive tasks so we can appreciate what we've done. We look back and see patterns. We take pride in quality work. And we do all of this in real time. We finish something, we move the sticky note which provides immediate feedback that we've accomplished what we set out to do.

CLARITY CALMS CARL

For as long as Carl can remember, his daughter Julie has been a gifted student. Although she's still in junior high, her guidance counselors have begun grooming her for early college admissions. She's on track to becoming a well-rounded candidate, one who'll appeal to a hyper-competitive admissions board. So in addition to good grades and solid test scores, Julie is now participating in community service, mulling over a run for student counsel, and even scheduling campus visits.

Until recently, Julie's bedroom walls were papered with glossy images of boy-band heartthrobs. Now they're covered with posters from universities and far away cities.

Julie is inspired. Her goal is obvious.

It's 3 AM and Carl's in bed, staring at the ceiling. For months he's been preoccupied, worried about finding a way to finance Julie's education. Right now his fears are amorphous, intimidating, and insomnia-inducing.

He remembers the quote he noticed earlier, pinned to Julie's bulletin board:

▶ **You are never given a dream without also being given the power to make it true. You may have to work for it, however. ~Richard Bach**

Work for it. Make it happen. *Perhaps it's better to confront this head-on and not wait for a miracle* he realizes. Carl sits up, feeling the spark of inspiration. He needs to make his goal obvious.

Julie has to do her part to ensure she'll get into a college of her choice. Now Carl realizes he needs a system to pay for it. Fortunately, time is on his side. He's at step one. He's made the decision. To get there, what does he have to do?

A heavy up-front plan is time consuming and rigid. While Carl's goal will stand the test of time, his assumptions will not. His income, job location, tuition costs, and Julie's desires might change. He needs a process that is flexible enough to respond to potential shifts in context.

But right now, Carl needs to act. He gets out of bed, goes to his den and above his Personal Kanban he writes his goal:

IN FOUR YEARS,
I WILL SEND JULIE TO UNIVERSITY

He steps back, stares at it, and lets out a wistful sigh. He thinks to himself *But how?*

Carl's not going to sketch out four years of work by writing a detailed plan on a Page-a-Day calendar. There are simply too many variables. But he has a goal and over the next four years he'll find opportunities to move towards it. This compels Carl to act.

Personally and professionally, we often get stuck in "analysis paralysis." We overcomplicate our situation, painstakingly planning to the minutest detail—details that, in the beginning, we have limited insight into. In the end, we allow the planning phase to stall the action phase.

Carl needs to come up with a few steps he can take immediately. He grabs a sticky note and makes a list of Julie's strengths and interests. He thinks it might be helpful to make these explicit so that together they can identify the best scholarship opportunities to pursue. On another sticky note he jots down a reminder to speak with his investment advisor and...hey, isn't one of his friends from college in the financial aid office at some university now? Carl makes a sticky note to talk to her as well.

He takes those sticky notes and populates his **READY** column with them. He pulls the investment advisor sticky note into **DOING,** and sends off a quick email.

He looks up at his Personal Kanban and his brain immediately understands that progress is being made towards his goal. Carl returns to bed happy, knowing he's being effective, knowing he's one step closer than he was just hours ago to financing his daughter's dream.

Carl no longer tosses and turns in bed, obsessing over the cost of his daughter's education. He doesn't worry that he didn't solve every issue tonight, because he's accepted that we never solve every issue. For the time being, useless worry has been dispelled. Carl can plan, he can be flexible, and he can achieve.

Carl has clarity.

VISUALIZE YOUR WORK

TO-DO LISTS: SPAWNS OF THE DEVIL

To-do lists: the last bastion for the organizationally damned. They're the embodiment of evil. They possess us and torment us, controlling what we do, highlighting what we haven't. They make us feel inadequate, and dismiss our achievements as if they were waste. These insomnia-producing, check-boxing Beelzebubs have intimidated us for too long.

toondoo.com

And they must be stopped.

An unyielding mashup of the pressing and superficial, to-do lists overload us mentally. They foster a mechanical, boring, dehumanizing approach to work; no sooner do we satisfy one task, we move thoughtlessly to the next. Let's face it, human beings don't like to be, well, *dehumanized*. We need context, something to-do lists don't provide.

In the absence of context, we have little information to guide our decisions. We can't see trade-offs, and with little insight into our options we fail to recognize our opportunities for fulfillment. Personal Kanban respects our humanity and the way we process work. Not only do we see priorities and the "done-ness" of our tasks, but we see how completing tasks impacts our options for future action.

By using Personal Kanban, we begin to set our own boundaries around the "games" of work and living. Games require actions in context. They are goal driven. There is a primary goal (to win) and several supporting goals (steps to complete in order to win). In a similar sense, Personal Kanban creates a defined, simple, yet rewarding game of our work: we have a primary goal (to live effectively), and supporting goals (to complete projects, to move sticky notes). We play this "game" on an ever-changing board (reflecting life's flow and context) which impacts outcome. In contrast, the to-do list "game" entails little more than completing tasks as quickly as possible: no flow from one action to the next, no suspense and ultimately, no reward.

Games should be energizing and evolutionary. We make a move, thus opening up a series of options. Our opponent makes a counter move. Some options close while others present themselves. Being able to visualize our work like this—as a system, as a game with intermediate and ultimate goals—enables us to become passionate about work itself. Life's trade-offs become explicit. We understand that if we're occupied with a mind-numbingly dull task one day, it's so we can engage in something enjoyable the next. We prioritize a trip to the butcher during Friday's rush hour because we know it means we can have a relaxing barbecue with our friends on Saturday afternoon. It's only when we can see our context and understand our options that we can effectively prioritize, work with our passions, and find purpose.

Personal Kanban vs. To-do Lists	
Personal Kanban	**To-do Lists**
Liberating	Anxiety Inducing
Adaptable	Static
WIP Limits	Overwhelming Tasks
Proactive	Reactive
Evolutionary	Stagnant
Experiential	Authoritarian
Collaborative	Autonomous
Meaningful / Enduring	Fleeting / Ephemeral
Options-based, Highlights Trade-offs	Single Points of Failure
Kinesthetic	Didactic
Finish & Remember	Check Off & Forget
Goal Refinement	No Goal Refinement
Prioritization On-the-fly	Brittle / Static
Continuous Improvement	Continuous Work
Effectiveness	Productivity
Contextual	Detached
Optimized for Clarity	Optimized for Cataloging
Narrative	Inventory
Bottleneck Aware	Bottleneck Ignorant
Flow Focused	Task Focused
Actionable	Overwhelming
Flexible	Prescriptive
Pull	Push

Learning vs. Reacting

Personal Kanban	To-do Lists
Liberating	Anxiety Inducing
Proactive	Reactive
Enduring	Ephemeral
Kinesthetic	Didactic
Flow Focused	Task Focused
Contextual	Detached
Optimized for Clarity	Optimized for Cataloging
Narrative	Inventory
Bottleneck Aware	Bottleneck Ignorant
Pull	Push

▶ **Tell me and I forget. Show me and I remember. Let me do and I understand.
~Confucius**

The most natural and effective learning results from doing. More than simply giving us experience, physically engaging in a task from its inception through to its completion teaches us the value and techniques of exercising successful options. We see our tasks, we become aware of their impacts, and we are reminded of their completion. This gives us the background vital for making future decisions.

To-do lists provide a context-free inventory of tasks that places us in reactive mode. We respond to work only as it arises and usually as its completion becomes dire. When we peruse our to-do list and ask ourselves *What's the biggest emergency?* that's not prioritization, it's reaction, and it's a self-fulfilling prophesy. The more we react, the more we will have to react to.

Personal Kanban transforms our work into a narrative giving us the context, the flow, and the decision points of a story. It doesn't give us a list of emergencies, but a series of causal relationships. Moving sticky notes, scrutinizing value streams, and holding retrospectives on a regular basis creates an enduring system. This system trains our brains to detect recurring patterns and causal relationships, such as tasks we enjoy, tasks that invite argument, and reasons for bottlenecks. From these types of observations we can proactively make decisions that increase the value of the options we exercise in the future.

Creating vs. Producing

Personal Kanban	To-do Lists
Actionable	Overwhelming
Collaborative	Autonomous
Options-based	Single Points of Failure
Flexible	Prescriptive
Effectiveness	Productivity
Pull	Push

To-do lists thrive in productivity-based, prescriptive environments, where the measure of quality is quantity. With to-do lists, you don't question *Why* or *How* a task is carried out, nor do you seek kaizen. You simply accomplish what you have to do, in the order it was received.

Personal Kanban fosters a creative and collaborative environment, where the measure of quality is effectiveness: doing the right work at the right time. The methods of work are never static; we constantly seek more effective ways of doing things (kaizen). To this end, visualizing work provides transparency, allowing team members to see what their peers are doing and identify opportunities for collaboration. By leveraging each other's time and talents, teams are able to expand individual and collective knowledge, ultimately expanding individual and collective options.

Evolution vs. Stagnation

Personal Kanban	To-do Lists
Adaptable	Static
Experiential	Authoritarian
Continuous Improvement	Continuous Work
Pull	Push

In order to apply what we learn, our practices need to keep pace with our evolving conditions and understanding. To-do lists assume our contexts are static. Without understanding why we're working, how we're working, and what options are within our reach, we end up working for the sake of working, rather than to appreciate how our efforts have a greater purpose.

Personal Kanban creates an adaptable system, one in which a kaizen becomes habitual. Based on our experience, we can modify our value stream or create entirely new Personal Kanban design patterns. Unlike to-do lists, where the goal is simply to satisfy tasks, Personal Kanban's goal is to visualize current work and our future options, allowing us to change our working methods as our options evolve.

PKFLOW TIPS

1. Manage work with flow and throughput, not time and capacity.

2. Like traffic, work doesn't fit, it flows.

3. Capacity is a spatial relationship, throughput is a flow relationship.

4. WIP limits can change with context.

5. Thoughtful prioritization and completion beats rigorous up-front planning.

6. Understanding our options is liberating.

CHAPTER 4
NATURE FLOWS

▶ Don't 'over-control' like a novice pilot. Stay loose enough from the flow that you can observe it, modify, and improve it. ~ Donald Rumsfeld

FLOW: WORK'S NATURAL MOVEMENT

Flow: The natural progress of work
Cadence: The predictable and regular elements of work
Slack: The gaps between work that make flow possible

The Tao of Physics. Flow. Freakonomics. Nonzero. Predictably Irrational. The Wisdom of Crowds. There's no shortage of best sellers expressing how the world is awash in both chaos and order. Much like the quote from Mr. Rumsfeld, these books suggest that observing a specific event is often less informative than observing a stream of events. It is precisely this flow which gives us context, and that context leads to clarity.

Whether it is in physics or economics or our personal lives, the further you delve, the more evident chaos becomes. In this book, we refer to that chaos as "variation." When you're in the vortex of that chaos, when it is all that you can see, you feel you're at its mercy. But when chaotic events are aggregated, they have a certain degree of predictability. Consider how it rarely floods in a 100 year flood plain. A flood can occur at any time, but we know there's a 1 in 100 chance it will come this year. It is this type of predictability on which we build our lives.

We shouldn't view our work as a series of isolated events. Static. Unique. Only vaguely related. The fact is, those presumably isolated events combine to build the story of our lives.

A few years ago, I had to force myself to complete a loathsome task: write a speaker's bio for a conference. My professional background is so diverse that I feared it would look disjointed, it sure felt that way to me. Over coffee, I complained about this to my companion, who asked me to describe what I assumed was a chaotic career. It went something like this:

Well, I studied psychology for a while and really loved it, but I didn't want to be a psychologist. So I went into urban planning, because as far back as I can remember I've been interested in cities—how they're built, how people live in them, work in them, navigate their lives in them. So for a decade I was an urban planner. I built rail transit systems, planned for growth management, built walkable neighborhoods. After a while I went into technology planning and software development for government, creating systems that helped government agencies collaborate internally or with other agencies or with the public. While doing that, I became interested in Agile software development practices, Lean manufacturing and social media and began getting projects in all three of those areas. That led to thinking about the way teams form and work together, how to motivate people to action, and what all that means to the individual.

That's when it became clear to both of us. My career did in fact have an underlying and pervasive current. Without ever setting out to do so, I managed to work in the creation of community on all levels.

The unifying theme, the "flow" of my career, was community.

Tonianne likes to say my nose was "too close to the canvas." Intently focused on the detail, I couldn't see the big picture. It was only when I took a step back and relaxed my concentration that I could finally appreciate my career in its entirety.

Donald Rumsfeld and Tonianne provide the same wisdom: step back, relax your focus, and observe. Personal Kanban enables us to do just that. It provides a mechanism to observe our work's context so that we can make informed decisions and plan with clarity.

CADENCE: WORK'S BEAT

The chassis of a car travel travels down an assembly line at a steady pace. It stops at regular intervals to have its engine installed or dashboard fitted or steering column mounted, then moves on to the next station and then the next, until the individual components yield a finished product. In manufacturing, the cadence that results is easy to detect. So easy in fact, that Warner Brothers set its cartoon assembly lines to Raymond Scott's iconic instrumental composition "Powerhouse," which features a series of energetic, repetitive riffs that have since become synonymous with the cadence of production. This is the rhythm of business.

Detecting and leveraging work's cadence is not confined to a factory setting. Consider how the tick-tock of a metronome helps a musician maintain a clean and consistent tempo, or how a coxswain's stroke meter ensures his crew's rowing is synchronized. Recognizing cadence in any workflow can help coordinate timing and streamline process, highlighting irregularities as they arise so they can be addressed at the source.

While it's often less mechanized, personal work also produces a cadence. When we visualize tasks as they travel through a value stream, we begin to detect an underlying rhythm in our workflow. We become attuned to its "beat," and can operate in unison with it. This cadence is reliable and reassuring, a reward in and of itself. It is a pattern that can be fine-tuned, allowing us to find and fix problems such as bottlenecks and disruptions, and determine pace, ultimately creating an expectation about our completion time.

Where the cadence of industry is often regimented, with a specific number and quality of beats per minute, personal work is often more frenetic, layered, and improvised.

SLACK: AVOIDING TOO MANY NOTES

▶ *Emperor Joseph II*: **Your work is ingenious. It's quality work. And there are simply too many notes, that's all. Just cut a few and it will be perfect.**

Mozart: **Which few did you have in mind, Majesty?**

~ Milos Forman's *Amadeus*

Revisiting the freeway analogy, consider what makes the roadway flow. Is it the cars, or the space between the cars? If there were no cars, there would be nothing to flow. If there was no space, the cars could not move. It's that balance between cars and open space that gives us flowing traffic.

That open space is called "slack." We need slack in our workflow, we need space to adjust. Without slack, we will overload. *Too many notes,* critiqued an overwhelmed emperor.

Pull too many sticky notes into your **TODAY** column and you set an expectation that all those tasks will be done that day. That overload will make you less responsive—

you'll be managing tasks like back-to-back meetings on your calendar. This will diminish your ability to pull, interrupt your flow, and impact your cadence.

PULL, FLOW, CADENCE, AND SLACK IN ACTION

During the pre-Colonial era, with the exception of turning the millstone, all tasks related to flour production were done manually. Raw material (wheat) was transported up several flights of stairs on the miller's back, then shoveled into a hopper. The step-by-step process was time-consuming and labor intensive, and with no means to separate debris or sift out the chaff, often resulted in dirty flour.

In the 18th Century, Oliver Evans improved the construction of the grist mill, streamlining the production process and transforming the milling industry. Lauded by both George Washington and Thomas Jefferson alike, his invention harnessed the energy of water and gravity to drive a continuous, more efficient system that produced higher quality flour. To power his mill, channels were dug and streams were dammed to get water to flow efficiently over wheels (just like the one on the cover of this book). Evans' grist mill was several stories high, equipped with a series of elevators, descenders, and conveyor belts that pulled grain to the top of the building, where it would cascade down a chute and into rotating millstones which would then grind the grain into flour.

The furrows between the millstones filled with grain and, as the stones turned, ground the grain into flour. However, if the furrows became too full they'd clog, literally grinding to a halt. As with a freeway, there is a point of optimal throughput—too much grain resulted in no further movement of the millstones. To ensure against this, the experienced miller closely monitored the amount of grain entering the millstones. Since they revolved at a regular rate, and grain fell out of the chute at a regular rate, the millstones likewise needed to be fed at a regular rate.

The miller's art was his careful judgment about the flow of the grain relative to the speed of the millstones. His finesse defined the flow of the work, essentially pulling the grain from its **READY** state into **DOING**.

That's right, the miller limited his WIP and optimized his slack.

Long before R.E. Olds and Henry Ford transformed mass production, Oliver Evans' fully automated grist mill revolutionized the assembly line process. From its inception it featured continuous flow and respected the value of limiting work-in-process. Each floor of the mill served a unique function, producing grain at a controlled, continuous, and consistent speed.

Adapting this concept, Olds and Ford built automotive assembly lines that moved product from one function-based station to the next. While productivity skyrocketed, their system was not without its shortcomings. Detroit's focus on production (productivity) over value (effectiveness) dehumanized the workplace. Production became more important than people and innovation suffered.

In Japan at Toyota, Taichi Ohno traced the disconnect between productivity and effectiveness to the very heart of the production system itself: the social system of the line workers. Ohno realized the issue wasn't necessarily the repetitive, mundane work associated with the assembly line but rather, how people related to their individual work, their teams, and the company as a whole. He discovered that in a push-based system, product travels down the line so regularly and work is so regimented, workers had no choice but to focus solely on their assigned task. Ohno wanted to expand line-worker's focus from simply producing a quality part to producing a quality vehicle. In order to do this, workers needed to be empowered to make business decisions and take responsibility for problems that arose beyond their station.

With its reputation for quality, post-war Japanese industry is greatly indebted to the management theories of W. Edwards Deming. Ohno's desire to enhance quality by increasing line-worker's clarity is the embodiment of Deming's call to "improve constantly and forever."[1] Deming inspired Ohno to create an informed work force that could make business-critical decisions without unnecessary management oversight. Case in point, this new "Lean" workforce was permitted to "stop the line." If line-workers detected a critical error, they could halt production and bring together a team to immediately correct the problem.

---

1   W. Edwards Deming, Out of the Crisis (Cambridge: MIT Press: 1982).

Increased access to information coupled with the ability to improve the company's processes led to marked increases in productivity, effectiveness, and job satisfaction. As a result, Toyota was able to reap significant benefits by respecting the line workers they had historically undervalued.

Intrinsic to Ohno's success was the kanban. While Toyota's organizational kanban doesn't quite resemble Personal Kanban, it has the same fundamental features: it visualizes work and tracks its flow, it allows line-workers to pull work when they have the capacity for it, and it highlights areas where improvements are needed. These elements helped Toyota achieve stability and sustainability.

Most management systems are put in place to stabilize a company (get control of backlog, balance the books) and promote sustainability (keep the company competitive, innovative, and profitable). Similarly, Personal Kanban helps you gain control of your backlog, understand your commitments, and pull work more effectively so that you too can achieve stability and sustainability while innovating.

Central to this—once again—is the concept of pull. Pull is essential for stability and sustainability. The more a system relies on a core mechanism to force action, the less sustainable it becomes. Push systems tend to cause bottlenecks by ignoring natural capacity. Work is released downstream whether or not the worker has the capacity to process it. In a push system, capacity problems are discovered after the fact. Work begins to pile up and, as it grows, can easily escalate into an emergency. Because it relies on committing to up-front guesses and does not anticipate the extra work, the push system can only react through costly and lagging responses like overtime, emergency hires, and delay.

A pull system operates according to flow: people take on work only when they have the capacity to do so. New work is pulled when prior tasks are completed, making the actual rate of completion explicit. In a pull system, managers know what their existing system is capable of processing, and they have a much better chance of predicting crunches before they occur. If a spike in activity is projected to occur in three months, a pull system can adjust for it ahead of time, avoiding costly, reactionary solutions.

BUSBOY WISDOM: THE NATURE OF PULL

I was 14 years old when I got my first job at The Village Inn Pancake House. For sub-minimum wage, I cleaned up people's half eaten pancakes, empty Coke glasses, and cigarette butts after they had their well-balanced breakfast. Like Personal Kanban, my busboy job was predicated on two primary rules: *Avoid speaking with the customers* and *Pull, never push, the bus cart.*

Late one afternoon, excited his shift was coming to an end, my co-worker was pushing his bus cart when he should have been pulling it. At an inadvisable speed, I should add. When the cart collided with the metal dividing strip between the dining area's carpet and the kitchen's linoleum, the front wheels got caught and the cart wiped out. The crash was deafening. Syrupy plates, dirty utensils, and dregs from half filled coffee mugs went airborne, leaving in their wake a filthy mess and horrified onlookers. I'll never forget the stunned expression on my co-worker's face, standing amidst the destruction he caused, teetering between baby tears and raucous teenage laughter. In the end, both impulses were satisfied.

Customers gasped *Oh my!*

Line cooks admonished *Pull, never push, the bus cart!*

The manager instructed calmly *Go home...and don't ever come back.*

What my fellow underage busboy learned that day was the difference between push and pull. Pushing tends to be a blind act; the initiator has little idea of the terrain situated before him. When you push, you're irrationally pushing your intent forward *whether your intent belongs there or not.* The dividing strip was a constraint. When the cart blindly hit the constraint, momentum halted abruptly and production turned into destruction.

In contrast, pulling is a rational act. The initiator is familiar with the terrain that lies ahead, and can gauge the amount of room in which to maneuver. Pulling allows for more nuanced intention. You're in the lead. You have clarity, you have control, and as a result your decisions are informed. Had my newly unemployed co-worker been pulling his cart, he would have seen the dividing strip and known to slow down, taking time to carefully guide the wheels over the ridge. With this foresight, the cart easily would have accommodated the constraint.

When you reach into your backlog and pull a task from **READY** into **DOING**, you're making a conscious choice based on the room you have in your WIP. You select a task that will unobtrusively merge into your workflow. While pulling won't make you omniscient, it will give you a better view of existing constraints and potential opportunity costs. In the end, your proverbial bus cart is much less likely to wipe out.

Most people find that their work is pushed onto them by others. When demands and obligations overload them, they are seldom afforded the opportunity to object. Management expects them to "step up to the plate." In those instances where workers attempt push back, they can't justify themselves because they don't have anything authoritative to point to that shows they're already overextended. In such situations, they need an arbitrator, a disinterested third party who can say *That person is overloaded, stop pushing work onto them.* In the absence of one, they're labelled whiners or worse, that they are not a "team player."[2]

Employees are routinely labeled under-performers, fired even, for not stretching themselves beyond their capacity. When management has little visibility into employee workload, they treat them as unconstrained resources capable of processing an infinite amount of work. People

---

2   *The team player concept is not a bad one, but in practice the moniker is often misused to single out individuals who make the rest of the group uncomfortable. The insidious thing about labeling an individual "not a teamplayer" is that it's simultaneously unprovable and universally condemning; it is meaningless and sinister and fodder for witch trials. When working with others, beware of undefined condemnations and be brave enough to ask what they mean when others issue them.*

aren't inexhaustible. They have a maximum throughput and, like Oliver Evans' grist mill, they'll grind to a halt if overloaded.

Personal Kanban makes our obligations explicit and transparent. As a physical manifestation of our workload, it gives us the ability to say *Look, this is my reality. I want to do a good job for you, but with all that's on my plate how can I possibly take on any more work?* Recognizing what your reality is and accepting work as you are able to complete it is the essence of pull.

REALITY CHECK

▶ **Reality is that which, when you stop believing in it, doesn't go away. ~Philip K. Dick**

Semper Gumby!

The world is highly variable. Natural disasters, unforeseen events, and the will of others can preclude the ability to pull on our own terms. Nevertheless, explicitly and realistically visualizing a seemingly overwhelming task load makes work more manageable.

Doing the right work at the right time requires us to optimize for the situation, to always be adaptable. If productivity is called for, optimize for productivity. If efficiency or effectiveness are called for optimize accordingly.

Pull when you can, be pushed when you must.

Don't become so enamored with the form of your Personal Kanban that you can't adapt to changing realities. Find the best visualization and working style to deal with overwhelming work in the moment.

PKFLOW TIPS

1. Life is a balance of order and chaos.
2. Patterns and contexts are often emergent. Don't lock yourself into plans before you have enough information.
3. Our actions today impact our choices tomorrow.
4. Pull, flow, and cadence give clarity to how we work and which options are appropriate to select.
5. Push is a blind act. Pull is informed.
6. Pulling is optimal, being pushed is inevitable. Semper Gumby. Always flexible.

CHAPTER 5

COMPONENTS OF A QUALITY LIFE

▶ **Decide what you want, decide what you are willing to exchange for it. Establish your priorities and go to work. ~H.L. Hunt**

Have you ever had one of those days? You know, the type where the entire universe seems to conspire against you? Of course you have. We all have. Tonianne sure did. She had a month of them, in fact. Here's her story.

~

It began when I scoffed at a friend's email. It contained my horoscope, which basically advised me to pull the blankets over my head and remain in bed for the next 30 days. That was the same day my car got towed, my dentist told me the pain I was experiencing was probably a sinus infection—or perhaps I needed a root canal, he couldn't determine which—and condensation from two of my air handlers, for the fourth time in a year, flooded three of my rooms.

Okay Universe, I can play your game.

With the proper cocktail of nitrous and narcotics, I knew I could handle any oral surgery that might be in my future. As for my car, it was eventually recovered. With several fresh scratches to commemorate the occasion. Within days of the flood however, the smell emanating from my walls became unacceptable. Mildew? Unlikely, as my persistent cough suggested, this was something serious. Not only could I sense it in my lungs, I'd read enough about the perils of toxic mold to know my environment was unhealthy. I needed to pursue this further. And so I did.

The walls were biopsied, and a furry green and black cross section confirmed what I suspected all along: mold, spore growth as high up as eight feet. The walls needed to come down immediately. My family had two hours to evacuate.

Okay I'm tough. I can handle this, I thought, assuming the worst was behind me.

On the fridge my calendar taunted me: the month wasn't even half over.

Donning respirators and wearing protective clothing, a hazmat team tented the contaminated areas and took samples. They were immediately followed by a demolition crew who tore down the walls, scrubbed the remaining beams, and ensured nothing toxic was left airborne. Within hours, my condo had been turned into a loft. Barely a wall was left standing.

Later that evening my husband and I returned to check on (what I loosely refer to as) the "progress." Up until this point I remained composed, in spite of the dust and disorder and electrical tape stuck to an 18th century English sideboard that's been in our family for generations.

Then I noticed the signs, they were everywhere: ASBESTOS.

Awesome. Universe: 100. Tonianne: 0.

Three days later, in the midst of all of this chaos, I began work with my dream client. Four days later my hacking cough was accompanied by a 104 degree fever, causing me to miss two days of work. Five days later my home was finally deemed (again, what I loosely refer to as) "inhabitable."

Upon our return, battling what I would later discover was a sinus infection, pneumonia, and a freshly broken rib, I assessed the damage.

I didn't know where to begin.

Furniture in disarray. A film of plaster particles everywhere. Drapes torn from their rods. New walls left unpainted. Phone, internet, and cable wires fried by the moisture. Electricity still not restored to the two rooms where wires had inadvertently been cut during demolition.

The to-do list pushed on us by these events seemed intermi-
nable. It included, but certainly was not limited to:

» *Make appointment with doctor to rule out sinus*
   infection / H1N1 / Mesothelioma / Bubonic Plague.

» *Call another dentist for second opinion RE: root*
   canal.

» *Get samples report from testing lab to see what we*
   were exposed to.

» *Schedule painters, pick up paint from Restoration*
   Hardware.

» *Follow-up with client.*

» *Send bedding and drapery for drycleaning.*

» *Beg housekeeper to work on a Saturday.*

» *Schedule appointment with Verizon.*

» *Schedule appointment with Comcast.*

» *Schedule appointment with electrician to restore*
   power.

» *Read mail.*

» *Get scratches on car buffed out.*

» *Call restorer to assess damage to sideboard.*

» *Submit insurance claim.*

» *Survey clothes, shoes, and other closet items exposed to*
   mold; see what's salvageable.

» *Research toxic mold.*

» *Research asbestos.*

Completely overwhelmed, I turned to the only thing I knew
could help me through this. No, not my mom. Or a martini.
Sure they could provide relief in the short term, but what I

needed was something to cut through the psychological clutter and ensure long-term results. I needed clarity. So I turned to my Personal Kanban.

Armed with sticky notes and a whiteboard, I planned my attack. I populated my **BACKLOG** *and began to prioritize. What moments earlier was a paralyzing, amorphous mass of I've-got-so-much-to-do-and-no-idea-where-to-begin was now a manageable series of discrete and actionable tasks. Most important however, was how my Personal Kanban focused my attention on those areas where the most long-term value could be affected (health-related tasks), rather than encourage me to tick off the easiest albeit least important tasks (having the car detailed or getting the sideboard restored).*

Understanding which tasks to pull and the physical act of pulling those sticky notes into **DONE** *lowered my existential overhead and made me feel awesome. And at that point in my life I needed all the awesome I could get.*

~

Personal Kanban provides not only a map, but a narrative of how we work, creating systems of instant understanding and rewards, learning and cognition, education and growth. We already touched upon the differences between productivity and effectiveness. We want to do good work, we want our efforts to have an impact. But we can't be effective without actually understanding our context. For this we need to understand not just the decisions we make, but how we come to make them.

METACOGNITION: A CURE FOR THE COMMON WISDOM

Productivity. Books, conferences, workshops, and coaches. Everywhere we turn we're reminded how our attempts to do more and work faster are failing miserably. Families require at least two incomes, children's schedules are as busy as a corporate CEO's. We're doing more than ever before to stay in the exact same place and it's exhausting.

Perhaps productivity isn't actually our goal.

We obsess over getting *stuff* done, rather than getting the *right stuff* done, and at the *right time.* We focus so intently on task completion that we lose sight of the work we're engaged in. We can't see our options, our history, or our opportunities for collaboration. In the long run, working like this isn't only counter-productive, it's anti-productive.

Without context, our workload confines and confounds us. Much like being caught up in a complex hedge maze, it separates us from the landscape of our work and truncates our horizon. We amble aimlessly from one task to the next, unable to see beyond a turn or two ahead. If we were to climb to the top of the garden maze and survey our surroundings, we could see turns, alternative pathways, dead ends and potentially, the path to victory. Similarly, having a panoramic view of our workload helps us understand how we work and make decisions. We can now describe and justify our choices to others.

Focusing on productivity is myopic. Effectiveness is our goal, and for that we need clarity. Clarity through visualization gives us the ability to choose the right work at the right time. But simply understanding our work is not enough. We also need to understand our decision-making processes, appreciate context, recognize relevancy, discern patterns, and choose between options. Clarity is not just understanding what we're doing, it's why and how we're doing it.

Personal Kanban is a metacognitive tool. It lets us take those bits of uncoordinated understanding (individual tasks) and situate them in a framework for systemic understanding (a value stream with clear options). This framework gives us insight into how and why we make decisions. Metacognition is knowing about knowing, it's becoming self-aware about how we choose what to do.

This is why seeing our is work helpful. Once visualized, our work takes the form of a narrative, plotting out the story of our daily lives with telling details such as actors, action, location, implications, and backstory. This narrative is told through the map of our work, which graphically depicts our work's contexts and relationships.

Without the map, our work is simply relegated to text, obscuring the story in rambling, confusing detail. When we attempt to describe the options and trade-offs with our work, we quickly devolve into:

I need to do these things and they relate to these people and need to be done by this time so I can get this result, but there are also these other things with other deadlines and other results and I know that I can do certain things in certain amounts of time and that this person is more forgiving than that person...

Text is unwieldy. For Personal Kanban, a picture is worth far more than a thousand words.

VISUALIZE YOUR WORK

WWW.TOONDOO.COM

PRODUCTIVITY, EFFICIENCY, AND EFFECTIVENESS

Productivity: You get a lot of work done, but is it the right work?

Efficiency: Your work is easily done, but is it focused for maximum effect?

Effectiveness: You get the right work done at the right time…this time.
Is this process repeatable?

Despite what those books, conferences, workshops, and coaches tell us, productivity should not be the ultimate measure of human potential. While Personal Kanban certainly helps us be more productive, it also helps us become more efficient and more effective.

Let's examine this more closely. Personal Kanban is:

- » A productivity tool: limiting our WIP helps us accomplish more.

- » An efficiency tool: focusing on our value stream encourages us to find ways to do more while expending less effort.

- » An effectiveness tool: making our options explicit leads us to make informed decisions.

We're all capable of having bursts of productivity, efficiency, and effectiveness—punctuated moments of heightened clarity, sense of purpose, and self-validation. Psychologist Abraham Maslow referred to these as "peak experiences"—revelatory or illuminating states of consciousness when we are operating at our best.[1] Popularly

---

[1]   Abraham H. Maslow, *Religions, Values, and Peak Experiences (New York, Penguin, 1994).*

we refer to this state as being "in the zone." These are instances when we recognize that right then, at that moment, there is a special quality for how our brain is working, how good we feel about our work, and how right our actions feel.

Peak experiences feel good.

We need to give ourselves credit for laying the groundwork for these peak experiences. If we don't acknowledge the things that put us in the zone, we dismiss peak experiences as happy accidents, mere flashes of unexpected brilliance. These experiences don't have to be a rarity, quite the opposite, in fact. Once we understand what causes peak experiences, we can increase their frequency and duration, creating "plateau moments." When we have clarity over our work and its purpose, plateau moments become common, eventually approaching a constant state of self-actualization. People in a self-actualized state are productive, efficient, and effective as a matter of course.[2]

Personal Kanban makes our work explicit. We see what we are doing, what trade-offs we have for future work, what we've done well historically, and what makes us happy. Equipped with this knowledge, we can interpret our options, weigh our commitments, and prioritize our tasks. Personal Kanban balances our productivity, efficiency, and effectiveness, making them three parts of the same kaizen machine. When we are truly productive, efficient, and effective we are more likely to enjoy whatever it is that we are doing, and feel compelled to do it better. This creates a virtuous cycle. We have clarity and are able to do good work. Feeling less stressed we do even better work. This is the heart of self-actualization.

---

2   *Maslow added a spiritual dimension to self-actualization that is beyond the scope of this book.*

DEFINING A GOOD INVESTMENT

In 2003, Gray Hill Solutions built an advanced traveler information system (ATIS) for a major metropolitan region. This web-based interactive traffic map was the product of a clear and executable vision, and it continues to serve millions of people daily. When I look at the website today, I can detect—as well as distinguish between—our team's bursts of productivity, efficiency, and effectiveness. I see the work, the processes, and the decisions; I see the disconnects and the peak experiences.

Over the course of two years, two separate companies attempted to build the ATIS, but failed to complete the job. We were brought in mid-project and expected to complete in a matter of months what others were given two years to do. Time was not on our side.

In addition to redesigning, building, and launching the website within a challenging time frame, our contract called for the creation of several reports, including a Detailed Design Document (DDD). Essentially a blueprint for software, the DDD was intended to guide the development process by providing a detailed description of what was to be built.

We were taking over a project that was already behind schedule and needed to start building immediately. The client pressed us to complete the web site first, and finish the DDD later—*six months after the site launched*. The DDD was a necessary document in its original time frame, but provided no value arriving after the website was built. This after the fact document was simply a requirement in their process. We begged the client to change the document to a user manual, or not require it at all. In the end, bureaucracy prevailed. We wrote the DDD after website delivery.

Upon its completion, we presented the 500+ page document to the client, who presumably put it in a drawer where it's languished ever since. While we can certainly see productivity in writing the DDD, there is very little evidence of the document's *effectiveness*. In the end, the only purpose it served was to satisfy a political requirement. Had effectiveness been the client's goal, the DDD would have been written as a user manual or, to save time and money, it would not have been written at all.

We all want to maximize the value we provide—to our clients, to our families, to posterity. Value here does not necessarily mean income or profit. There is little correlation between emotional satisfaction and monetary compensation. Professional, creative and emotional satisfaction often result from other types of compensation. To feel truly successful, fulfilled, or self-actualized, we need to feel pride in our work.

Ultimately, our sense of purpose rests on the knowledge that our labor has utility and our efforts have an impact. While millions of commuters continue to utilize our traffic website daily, the DDD is useful to no one. The report is illustrative only of productivity—for us as professionals productivity wasn't as rewarding as effectiveness.

In contrast, the website was an excellent example of effectiveness, with a small team creating a highly rewarding product of obvious value. Mere productivity is never a good investment. Effectiveness is far more valuable.

REALITY CHECK

Our goal is to strike a balance between being productive, efficient, and effective. *What tasks or goals would you pull to achieve happiness? To exercise your talents and expertise? To bring you satisfaction and joy? What tasks reward you simply by doing them? What pushes you to do things that don't make you happy? What trade-offs are necessary to achieve balance? How can you remove friction from your life?*

Personal Kanban helps us process these questions. There is no final answer. There is no right answer. But more happiness is attainable. Understanding our strengths, formulating goals that make the best use of our strengths, and setting ourselves up for success—that can be accomplished with clarity.

PKFLOW TIPS

1. Visualization dispels fear.

2. Clarity lets us improve not only our decisions, but our decision-making processes.

3. Productivity without effectiveness is waste.

4. Notable bursts of effectiveness are the heart of a peak experience.

5. Repeatable peak experiences enable kaizen.

6. Understanding our work and how we prioritize allows us to find balance between push and pull.

CHAPTER 6
FINDING OUR PRIORITIES

▶ **If you know the enemy and know yourself you need not fear the results of a hundred battles. ~Sun Tzu**

For years I had a goal to walk at least 10,000 steps each day. There was a pedometer in my pocket at all times, and I would do whatever it took to meet my objective. Even if I was on a phone call, I would step away from my desk, and walk up a few flights of stairs or circle my office building while talking, just to watch the numbers on the pedometer rise.

As a result, I was healthy and fit.

At one point the battery in my pedometer died. I neglected to replace it for several months, not really thinking it was much of an issue until I was midway through writing this book. Planted behind my laptop for twelve to fifteen hours each day, I wasn't getting up and walking around *at all*.

My mood and my health suffered.

My pedometer was my measure, my motivator, my visual control. It let me know at any given moment how close I was to my goal and the number of steps I needed to reach it. So long as I had access to the control there was an immediate reward for action (satisfaction), and an immediate punishment for inaction (disappointment). My pedometer was pocket clarity. With it, I prioritized walking.

Without it, my steps were no longer explicit; the exercise value of walking became immeasurable. So long as it was without batteries, I unconsciously deprioritized walking because there was no control to satisfy. The visual control kept me honest.

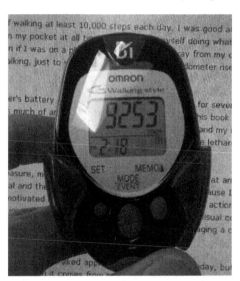

Now for the sake of argument, I am an "expert" walker. I know the biometrics, the footware, the technology. I've walked in the rain and the snow, in nearly every state in the U.S. and on three continents. Clearly I should be able to estimate my total steps. Take today for example, I was extremely active, and so I estimate my steps to be close to 14,000. Without a visual control, even an educated guess remains just a shot in the dark. Taking the pedometer with its fresh new battery from my pocket, I am immediately proven wrong. We can see it: 9,253 steps. The pedometer shows me what "right" is.

Managing a concept is merely guesswork. In the absence of a visual control we don't estimate, we guess. Our guesses are based on what we *think* is insight gained from our experiences, when in actuality they are based on incomplete and inadequate information shaped by our hopes and our fears. Optimistic and happy, I overestimated my steps. With no objective measure, our emotions are the only metric we have to rely on.

Unfortunately, this is how most businesses, teams, and individuals measure their work. Many of us consider ourselves experts in our craft and so we estimate based on our memory. We remember how long it took us to perform a task and plug that estimation into our plan. Educated guesswork is no substitute for thoughtful observation. Estimates often project our dreams, rather than reflect our reality.

Real, informed estimates for future work take into account how we worked in the past as well as how often we were derailed. If we complete a task in two hours, that does not mean we can replicate that task's completion four times in an eight hour work day or 20 times in a 40 hour work week. There is a difference between how long it took us to accomplish a task in the past and how much time we allocate for it the next time. Our context is always changing. To account for variability, interruptions, and innovation, we need to factor in slack time. Sometimes that two hour task will take an hour and a half, sometimes it will take upwards of four hours. That's the nature of work. We need flexibility to adjust what we're doing to respond to our context.

STRUCTURE, CLARITY, AND OUR ABILITY TO PRIORITIZE

In his book *Predictably Irrational: The Hidden Forces That Shape Our Decisions*, MIT professor Dan Ariely describes an experiment in options.[1] He assigned each of his three classes a different type of deadline for their papers:

» One class was given firm deadlines.

» One class was allowed to set their own personal deadlines ahead of time.

» One class had no deadlines, and could submit their papers at any time during the semester.

In all three cases, late papers were penalized. Dr. Ariely found papers submitted by the class with dictated due dates had the best grades, while papers submitted by the class that set their own deadlines came in second. As it turned out, the class with neither dictated nor self-imposed deadlines received the worst grades.

With the freedom to submit their papers at their convenience, shouldn't students have been able to better schedule research, writing and editing time? *Shouldn't they have excelled in this state of pull nirvana?*

Dr. Ariely attributes this disconnect to procrastination, and hypothesizes that deadlines are the best cure. However, his experiment also illustrates how clarity is the engine of effective prioritization.

---

1   Dan Ariely, Predictably Irrational: The Hidden Forces That Shape Our Decisions (New York: Harper Perennial, 2008), p.141-147.

Maximum clarity. Maximum prioritization.

Students with dictated (pushed) deadlines were able to prioritize their work. They respected the concept of a firm deadline and understood the ramifications for missing it. As such, they had clarity over what was expected from them. This clarity forced prioritization and was a system the students were familiar with.

Some clarity. Some prioritization.

A self-imposed deadline provides some of the clarity of a dictated deadline. These deadlines most likely resulted from students analyzing their other courses' dictated (pushed) deadlines, and then figuring out the best time for them to complete their papers for Dr. Ariely. The problem was that self-imposed deadlines did not seem as serious. They were not external and therefore could be deprioritized, but not entirely ignored.

No clarity. No prioritization.

Lack of any deadline equated to a lack of structure, and ultimately a lack of clarity. Deadlines for other classes took precedence over Dr. Ariely's deadline-free class. In theory, the removal of deadlines should have created a pull system for the students—they could work on Dr. Ariely's papers at their leisure. The problem may not have been with the concept of pull, or students' procrastination, but instead with an unfamiliar pull system in a push-driven environment.

While having the capability for efficiency and effectiveness, pull was out of context for Ariely's students.
Accustomed to the dictated deadlines of the push system,
they had no way to integrate the differing demands of the
two.

What these students needed was a value translator, a
visual control to bridge requirements of their push classes
with those for Dr. Ariely's pull class.

Personal Kanban's visual nature would have made their
context obvious. In this case, Dr. Ariely's students demonstrated that the deadline was a proxy for clarity. The
papers for his classes were no less important, but students
needed a familiar trigger like a deadline to compel them
to action. As the deadlines were relaxed, a different form
of trigger was required.

Visualizing their work would have prompted students
to pull Dr. Ariely's work even when push-based deadlines loomed. In all likelihood, students were plowing
though all their papers at the end of the term anyway.
Personal Kanban would have rewarded prioritization of
Dr. Ariely's papers earlier in the semester, when their
workload was still light and deadlines few.

SMALLER, FASTER, BETTER: CONTROLLING TASK SIZE AND LIMITING WIP

▶ **Plans are useless, but planning is indispensable. ~ Dwight D. Eisenhower**

Lots of productivity tools recommend breaking work into small chunks. Smaller tasks are easier to comprehend and complete. When you take on smaller tasks, you've invested less time in the product, reducing the cost of change and failure.

On its own, controlling task size serves as a poor man's WIP limit. Simply making tasks smaller isn't enough; small, unmanaged tasks can accumulate and overwhelm. Reducing task size is only truly effective when coupled with limiting WIP: tasks are completed sooner, results become measurable, and existential overhead is kept to a minimum. Therefore, we should focus on limiting WIP and completing tasks first, and make task size reduction a secondary concern.

While we want to reduce task size to make our work more manageable, we shouldn't become obsessive with or enslaved by the process. We want to avoid becoming mired in detail and committing prematurely. People uniformly spend too much time estimating the size, costs, and impacts of their work. They overplan up front and as context changes, they find themselves endlessly modifying their original assumptions. Planning should occur with minimal waste; it shouldn't become overhead.

LIMIT YOUR WORK-IN-PROGRESS

With Personal Kanban we're in a perpetual state of planning. It becomes part of our work's flow. You watch the narrative of your work take shape—you see context, you see natural progression, you see options and from this insight you can make truly informed decisions.

A project's context, tasks, and subtasks are subject to change. Plan, estimate, and break down tasks at the last responsible moment. We want to time our planning for when it can be the most effective—when we have sufficient information, or when we have no other choice than to begin work.

PRIORITIZATION IN THEORY AND PRACTICE

▶ **No battle plan survives contact with the enemy. ~ Carl von Clausewitz**

Regardless of whether we're managing a multinational corporation or our family's weekly schedule, options provide the foundation for prioritization. Prioritization represents a decision of value: we canvass existing options and choose the ones ready for immediate attention or attention in the near future.[2] Prioritization entails exercising an option or simply determining the option is worthy of being exercised.

This section offers some simple techniques to help you prioritize effectively. Ideally, prioritization is context-driven. Context and options for personal tasks shift con-

---

2   There is substantial science behind real options theory, which is the basis for options trading and some avenues of decision-making. Real options theory has potent lessons for personal work, but this is beyond the scope of this book.

stantly, prioritization methods need to be tailored to suit the situation. Remaining flexible enough to adapt and prioritize on-the-fly is key.

Why?

We want to do the right thing, right now. We want to exercise our options as well as we possibly can. While some options have undeniable immediate value, there are others we should exercise for long-term effectiveness. We prioritize based on profit, health, happiness, family, altruism and a host of other fairly complex criteria. With an eye for both short-term and long-term effectiveness, we avoid the traps of unchecked productivity and endless planning.

Just as Carl didn't need to figure out in one night every step in his four year plan to finance Julie's education, we too are better served by allowing projects to unfold as context demands. This doesn't mean you should put off thinking about the future. It does mean you should take on work thoughtfully, in chunks you can handle, and be prepared to revise your original plans when context demands.

There are countless ways to organize your backlog. The following visualizations are just a handful to get you started. They will help you see your options, allowing you to remain flexible enough to deal with life's shifting realities.

URGENCY & IMPORTANCE

In late 2009, Personal Kanban user Eva Schiffer wrote to us:

> *I have just erased my to-do list and transformed it in something kanban-like. My own to-do list format, that always worked well for me, had 4 categories:*
>
> » *Important and urgent*
>
> » *Important, less urgent*
>
> » *Less important, urgent*
>
> » *Less important, less urgent*
>
> *That helps me a lot because I normally love the less important, less urgent tasks, and while they often lead to really interesting creative outcomes, it is important for me to keep procrastination at bay and make sure that I don't just impress myself with the number of tasks performed, but also do those things that are most urgent and / or important.*

Eva maps out her backlog by assigning tasks to relevant quadrants, helping her identify the functional context of her work and facilitate prioritization. Adapted from a system used by General Dwight D. Eisenhower and later popularized by Stephen Covey, the "Time Management Matrix" highlights the relative urgency and importance of our tasks.[3]

---

3   Stephen Covey, Seven Habits of Highly Effective People (New York: Free Press, 1989) and First Things First (New York: Free Press, 1994).

Covey defines the activities that belong in each quadrant, offering recommendations for which are the best use of our time and which to avoid. While we appreciate his system for the way it helps visualize some key work contexts, we find that such rigid definitions deter us from engaging in activities with unknown or highly variable value.

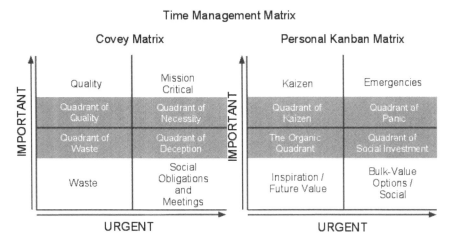

Time Management Matrix

When combined with your Personal Kanban, the Time Management Matrix adds another dimension of context to your backlog, creating an options valuation and kaizen matrix that is positive and proactive. To describe this new twist, let's explore how Personal Kanban extends Covey's interpretation.

URGENT AND IMPORTANT

Classic Covey - The Quadrant of Necessity: This quadrant reflects tasks that are both urgent and important, responding to mission-critical events such as unforeseen emergencies, approaching deadlines, angry client demands, and escalated honey-dos. This is the quadrant where our expertise and personal value are often optimized, where Covey suggests we place our best workers. These high-stress tasks often have immediate and obvious payoff.

The Personal Kanban Difference - The Quadrant of Panic: While Covey's methodology focuses on the content of this quadrant, Personal Kanban exposes and questions why this stress-inducing quadrant has contents at all. *Are the urgent and important tasks preventable? Are they in response to an emergency? Were they caused by a certain behavior? Do they tend to recur?* This quadrant should be limited to those tasks which are unavoidably urgent and important, and not just what we've procrastinated on or deprioritized to the point that they've become emergencies.

Tasks whose status escalates into Urgent and Important should be flagged for a retrospective. Personal Kanban wants us to put our rank and file workers in this quadrant and devote our best workers instead to the Important but not Urgent quadrant which, in the long run, can greatly reduce activity in this quadrant. Our heroes don't belong here. Our focus should be on avoiding emergencies, not reacting to them.

IMPORTANT BUT NOT URGENT

Classic Covey - The Quadrant of Quality and Personal Leadership: This quadrant reflects tasks that are important but not urgent, quality-related activities such as enhancing skills, removing bottlenecks, and ensuring effectiveness. This is the quadrant where potential improvements or kaizen events are realized.

The Personal Kanban Difference - The Quadrant of Kaizen: This quadrant contains quality-related tasks—the time and effort you spend here is an investment in future quality. Elevating and prioritizing this quadrant is the essence of kaizen. Since these tasks provide future rather than immediate results, they are often left deprioritized in favor of Urgent and Important tasks. This quadrant should be your focal point, because the more you ignore the tasks within, the more they'll gravitate towards the panic quadrant. This quadrant is the antidote for panic.

URGENT BUT NOT IMPORTANT

Classic Covey - The Quadrant of Deception: This quadrant contains tasks that are externally imposed, socially-based activities such as telephone calls, visitors, and meetings. Covey recommends limiting tasks in this quadrant because they are deceptive: they appear to be productive, but in actuality are a waste of our time.

The Personal Kanban Difference - The Quadrant of Social Investment: The Urgent but not Important distinction is subjective. Tasks in this quadrant can certainly be waste, but how can you be sure?

In many instances, the actual value of telephone calls, visitors, and meetings that may veer off-topic can go unrealized until well into the future. You might meet with eight potential clients over the course of eight dinners, and hear from none of them until one calls six months later. That call results in one of their contacts giving you a contract worth millions. So were the other seven meetings a waste of your time? Should you have had only one meeting? How could you have possibly known in advance which of the eight was the "meeting of value?"

Each of those meetings was an investment in a portfolio of social options.

NOT URGENT AND NOT IMPORTANT

Classic Covey – The Quadrant of Waste: The actions in this quadrant are deemed "time wasters," they are those "pleasant activities" that provide no apparent value and distract us from being productive.[4] Covey strongly recommends avoiding actions that fit into this quadrant.

The Personal Kanban Difference – The Organic Quadrant: It's your life. You define your pastimes, you define your waste, you define your value. Some people consider playing online games or surfing the Web to be counterproductive. Yet there are endless stories of marriages resulting from World of Warcraft and business opportunities presenting themselves through Twitter. This quadrant can be one of assumed waste, or it can be one for actions you find pleasant (*pleasant is good!*) that may evolve into more tangible future value.

Think of this quadrant as a garden where options can germinate and grow. There are many seeds, a whole lot of fertilizer, and rich soil. Covey simply acknowledges the fertilizer. This quadrant is where experimentation occurs, where we find new options previously unimagined. Options are not always discovered during planning, they often come from happenstance. In the other three quadrants you will find work; here you will find inspiration. This is the organic quadrant.

---

4   Stephen Covey, *7 Habits of Highly Effective People, (New York: Free Press, 1989) p. 151.*

LIVE YOUR OWN LIFE

▶ **Time you enjoy wasting, was not wasted. ~ John Lennon**

Covey's Time Management Matrix specifically instructs which quadrants to prioritize and which to avoid. While some quadrants have a tendency to dominate, all four are integral to a balanced life. With Personal Kanban, these quadrants function as an ecosystem—each capable of contributing both value and waste. In order to optimize the matrix, it is necessary to balance our priorities, spending an appropriate amount of time staving off emergencies, engaging in improvement, and allowing time for healthy social interactions and exploration of new options.

Priority Filters

While the Time Management Matrix gives us a way to categorize our work, fixed quadrants don't reveal flow. Covey undervalues the lower two quadrants, contending the tasks contained within have little or no value. We would argue that their value becomes apparent over time.

Value drives how we prioritize: we choose tasks with higher value first. Sometimes our priorities become apparent through flow and not through fixed quadrants. Both value and prioritization evolve with context.

Corey Ladas' Priority Filter creates a flow system of prioritization.[5] "Buckets" with limited capacity show tasks trickling down from your backlog into **DOING**. Each successive bucket has less capacity, cre-

---

5   Corey Ladas, Scrumban: Essays on Kanban Systems for Lean Software Development, (Seattle: Modus Cooperandi Press, 2008) p. 163.

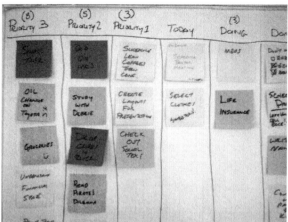

ating the need to analyze the current priority when pull-ing a task. Taking into consideration how our context changes throughout the day, the Priority Filter helps us focus on priorities without committing us to any actions outright.

The Priority Filter provides you with a deep visual distil-lation of the high priority tasks in your backlog. Unlike Covey's Time Management Matrix, the Priority Filter does not assign value judgments to your actions, nor does it dictate which tasks should be addressed first. Instead, it is context-driven and flexible, allowing you to see your priority assumptions at any given moment.

GTD Prioritization

Created by David Allen, "Getting Things Done" (GTD) is an organizational method to control backlogs and cap-ture ideas for future work.[6] Like Personal Kanban, GTD improves your understanding of how and why work is conducted.

---

6   David Allan, Getting Things Done (New York: Penguin, 2002).

GTD relies on lists and folders with review disciplines to record and manage massive active and inactive backlogs. Think of GTD as a wine cellar for your ideas. It can coherently store a wide array of options that will mature over time.

Both Personal Kanban and GTD seek to reduce the analysis paralysis so often caused by an overwhelming amount of work. Combined, these two methodologies create a system where large, long-term projects can be stored in GTD folders and incorporated into your Personal Kanban when they are ready to process effectively.

Task Types: Using Color and Shape

Just as geographic maps use color and shape to communicate certain types of information, so too can your Personal Kanban. Whether you're using a whiteboard, a flip chart, or a computer-based system, color and shape are deceptively simple yet robust ways to differentiate between tasks, projects, collaborators, or priority. You can even use them to call out patterns, such as tasks you consistently procrastinate on or that tend to require outside assistance.

My distaste for administrative work is the stuff of legends. If it involves bookkeeping, filing taxes, or submitting claims of any sort, I'm probably going to let those obligations accumulate until the last responsible minute (or slightly after), complaining the entire time. So on my Personal Kanban I assign such loathsome tasks bright orange sticky notes.

While not all of us drag our heels on unwelcome tasks, we certainly might *conveniently deprioritize* them. By assigning them a color or shape that stands out, we are confronted with them piling up in our backlog. Being able to visualize these tasks shows us the weight of their existential overhead, until finally we have to bite the bullet and process a bunch of them *en masse*.

Use a little creativity to call attention to certain kinds of tasks that may require special attention. Sometimes a little visual reinforcement is the push to action we need.

EXPERT: METRICS IN PERSONAL KANBAN

▶   **You can observe a lot by just watching. ~ Yogi Berra**

Metrics help us gauge our progress, validate our performance, measure proximity to our goals, and show us where our actions can be improved. Progress, as we've seen, is relative to and a matter of context. Metrics should reflect our context, revealing the difference between expected and actual progress. Carl wanted to see how close he was to sending his daughter to college. Tonianne wanted to see how close she was to reclaiming a healthy household. With Personal Kanban, they could each track what was done, and what remained toward reaching their respective goals. This type of situational knowledge is probably the most important metric we have.

Situational knowledge is seeing the road, metrics are the gas gauge. Visualizing work combined with metrics provides a full understanding of the current situation. Well-chosen metrics test hypotheses, allowing us to track past events and foresee potential outcomes.

Metrics gathered but not used are waste, so choose them with care. Ensure they are actively and thoughtfully proving an hypothesis. If you sense a change is occurring and want to prove it, establish a target, devise a metric, begin to track it, and continue to measure for as long as that measurement is relevant.

Note: Don't fall prey to "metric-blindness," where you rely too heavily on metrics without having good situational knowledge.

Personal Kanban not only tracks workflow, it generates a wealth of actionable data: it offers insight into the root causes of performance shortfalls and successes, creating an opportunity to alter bad behaviors, codify proven processes, set realistic goals and with time, systematically

LIMIT YOUR WORK-IN-PROGRESS

improve performance. This insight can result from quantitative or even more experiential measures.[7]

Personal Kanban is a light system with two rules and two rules only: *Visualize your work* and *Limit your WIP*. For those who would like to extend the value of their Personal Kanban, the following suggested metrics can help you analyze your work.

Metric One: Your Gut

▶ **The only real valuable thing is intuition. ~ Albert Einstein**

Transparency into work sensitizes you to its patterns. With Personal Kanban, you intuitively begin to look for ways to improve work's flow. This is your gut, your sixth sense, your instinct. This is your first line of defense.

Why are we now suggesting that intuition is an acceptable metric, when just a few pages back we demonstrated how unreliable subjective measures can be? The answer is precision. While our gut is no replacement for our pedometer's ability to determine the exact number of steps we've taken, it can tell us when we've traveled far. Similarly, our intuition can tell us when something needs to be improved. These impulses are what we base our hypotheses on. Our gut notices a pattern, our brain forms an hypothesis, our Personal Kanban validates or rejects it. From there we can make improvements.

We don't act on something without noticing it. Hopefully we can spot a potential improvement before it is picked

---

7   *For cumulative flow diagrams and other measures, see personalkanban.com.*

up by numbers, charts and graphs. Don't downplay intuition. Part of kaizen is creating positive change without over-thinking it. By reflex. By your gut.

Metric Two: The Process Laboratory

▶ **If you employed study, thinking, and planning time daily, you could develop and use the power that can change the course of your destiny.**
~ W. Clement Stone

Back in Chapter 2, we introduced the **TODAY** column. Adding a **TODAY** column to the basic Personal Kanban **READY -> DOING -> DONE** value stream is more than a way to hyper-prioritize your work, it also serves as an evaluative measure.

Regulating our physiological functions, our circadian rhythms force us to respect the concept of a day. Upon waking, we have a natural tendency to mentally organize the hours ahead of us. We quickly set aside a group of tasks and think *This is what I want to accomplish on this day.* It then becomes a goal. Not only do we track the progress we've made on tasks we *expect* to accomplish in a single day, we also get a baseline against which to measure how much work we *actually* accomplish.

Just as we added a **TODAY** column to see if we met or came close to meeting our daily targets, we can also introduce columns that visualize certain hypotheses about our successes or failures.

During a recent client engagement, there was an individual in the organization who wielded so much control over the fate of a funding request that he was menacingly referred to as "the gatekeeper." To protect the innocent, we'll call this person Reginald. A notorious stickler for detail, Reginald tries so hard to control costs that in the end he actually creates waste.

If you submitted a 100 page project plan but failed to include a minor expense on page 97, Reginald will kick the entire document back to you rather than ask for the number in question, incorporate it into the document, and approve the request.

While it would take him less than five minutes to ask you for that number, that document—once corrected and resubmitted—cycles to the bottom of Reginald's inbox. By the time he gets around to reviewing it, he begins at page one.

Delays like these are time consuming and costly. They contribute to WIP and ultimately welcome error. Working like this is not sustainable.

While figuring out a value stream for my client, she explained her biggest problem was Reginald. Every time she needed to get something done, the funding request would languish on his desk. *It's a shame we can't just put HIM up on the board so everyone could see how much HE costs the company in delays* she lamented.

Hmm...now there's a thought.

So we included a column on the team's Personal Kanban labeled **FUNDING REQUEST REVIEW**. Now when documents are held up, the reason for their inactivity is apparent to everyone, including Reginald.

What was previously a universal yet unprovable annoyance is now an hypothesis that can be confirmed and addressed. By visualizing Reginald's actions, his impact on the team is made obvious: *Tasks are stalled three days on average by that guy's obsessive need to focus.*

Metric Three: The Subjective Well Being Box

▶ **Happiness is not something ready made. It comes from your own actions.**
~ Dalai Lama

During Modus Cooperandi's 2009 year-end retrospective, we had a revelation:

> *Doing things you don't enjoy reduces your effectiveness.*

This includes tasks you aren't particularly good at, projects you find unfulfilling, and working with individuals you dislike. It's not just about not wanting to do things that aren't fun, mind you. Unenjoyable tasks increase existential overhead. When it comes time to do something you dread, you become anxious, irritable, and less thoughtful. There are legitimate opportunity costs in doing things you don't enjoy.

Let's take Bob, for instance. Bob really hates to do his taxes and it's time for his quarterly submittal. He knows from past experience that it takes him about an hour to submit his forms online. He figures if he makes $75.00 an hour with his consulting business, and an accountant charges $150.00 to file his taxes, it's more cost-effective to just suffer through the process and file them on his own. But what Bob fails to consider is that he spends an hour bemoaning the process before he even sits down at his desk. He then spends another hour recovering, and then for a week or so afterwards worrying if he filed them correctly, losing sleep and gaining a few extra grey hairs at the thought of IRS agents knocking at his door. In the end, all that time and stress adds up to far more than his accountant would have charged him.

Next quarter, Bob should seriously consider getting an accountant.

Which brings us to an easy metric: the Subjective Well-Being (SWB) Box. "Subjective well being" is a psycho-

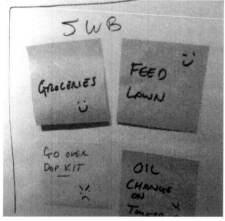

logical concept and a qualitative measure that gauges an individual's current mental state by asking them. If we ask you *How are you feeling?* and you respond *Pretty darn good!* then that's basis for your subjective well-being.

The SWB Box helps us identify what exactly impacts our mood so that we can begin to optimize for "pretty good," "good" or even "great." It also lets us put into perspective those onerous tasks we simply don't like doing. With the SWB Box, we can finally establish that these annoyances are simply tasks, and not a way of life. We'll get them done, understanding something better is just around the bend.

How this works is simple. First, draw a box on or near your Personal Kanban (you could even use a physical box). When you complete a task and it moves you to an extreme—leaving you giddy or downright annoyed— annotate whether it was a positive or negative experience, and why. Then move that task to the SWB Box.

With every task you deposit into the SWB Box ask yourself: *Why did I like or dislike this task? Did the people or resources involved impact my mood positively or negatively? Is this a task I should delegate in the future?*

When it comes time to hold a retrospective, revisit the contents of the SWB Box, grouping together tasks with similar comments. Don't discard the contents of your SWB Box until you begin to recognize patterns. When you do, consider:

» When to refuse work.

» When to delegate work.

» What changes can help ensure success.

» Which processes you might want to recreate.

» What your career options really are.

» How to balance family, career, recreation, and personal development.

It might take several retrospectives until patterns begin to present themselves. Be patient. They have the potential to provide insight into the way you work, and illuminate the things that make you happy, so don't lose sight of them.

LIMIT YOUR WORK-IN-PROGRESS

Don't be surprised to discover that the things you enjoy are the things you are also good at. When you find your strengths, you can nurture them. The more you do what you are good at, the more you enjoy your work, and the better you become at the work you enjoy.

Metric Four: Time

▶ **A man who carries a cat by the tail learns something he can learn in no other way. ~ Mark Twain**

If you want to get all statistical about Personal Kanban, this is the step to do it in. When you create a sticky note, include the date of creation (Born), the date you pull it into **READY** (Begin), the date you began working on it (WIP), and when you are finished, the date you pull it into **DONE** (Done).

These four data points can be used to analyze your work's "lead time" and "cycle time." Lead time for Personal Kanban is the amount of time it takes a task to travel from your backlog to completion. Cycle time is the amount of time it takes a task to travel from **READY** to **DONE**.

While both metrics bring value (like how long home improvement tasks take or how often you work with crazy Larry), understanding how much work you are capable of processing—your throughput—helps measure your efficiency, and so cycle time is probably the metric to begin with. It tells us how long it actually takes us to complete a task, helping us better understand the accuracy of and assumptions behind our estimates.

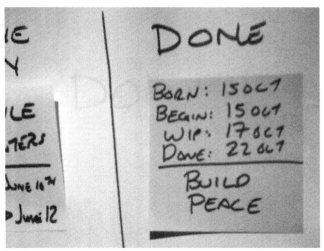

By giving us a more realistic idea of our throughput, cycle time can also help us refine our WIP limit. Just remember, personal work is subject to a high degree of variation, so analyze and apply these numbers judiciously. If you measure cycle time for all your tasks, you will likely end up with meaningless statistics that aggregate times for tasks as disparate as "Make dinner reservations at Zaytinya" and "Move to Chile."

Go Forth and Measure

Equipped with these metrics, you can revisit specific tasks and begin to evaluate. There's always an explanation for those tasks which defy our expectations, tasks which burden us. Whether it's procrastination on our part or factors beyond our control, there's always something and, thankfully, quite often that something can be fixed.

VISUALIZE YOUR WORK

PKFLOW TIPS

1. Expertise is no substitute for observation and measurement.

2. Clarity drives prioritization, completion, and effectiveness.

3. Metrics don't have to be difficult.

4. Visual controls remove guesswork.

5. Real-time flexiblity beats rigid up-front planning.

6. Happiness may be the best measure of success.

CHAPTER 7
STRIVE FOR IMPROVEMENT

We breed dragons so our heroes can slay them.

We love our heroes. We invest our time, our money, and our faith in their ability to prevail under extraordinary circumstances. We exaggerate their role and mythologize their talent at the risk of undervaluing our own. Lazy managers are especially notorious for this. Rather than develop and nurture the capabilities of existing staff, hastily and habitually they seek the services of heroes. Judging by a quick scan of online career sites laden with superlative-heavy postings seeking social media "gurus," IT "ninjas," and marketing "rock stars," hero worship is alive and well and practiced in a human resources departments near you.

Take A-List coders, for example. Characterized by the (alleged) quality of the code they write, the (alleged) speed at which they work, and their (alleged) ability to deliver exactly what their bosses ask for, A-list coders are the holy grail of software design. Rumors of their miraculous powers notwithstanding, "A-List" is merely a convenient and unscientific distinction: there is no certification for or test to become an A-List coder. In spite of this, there seems to be a legitimate group of coders who routinely outperform others in stressful situations.

So who are these people and are their deeds really heroic?

At Gray Hill Solutions, we too sought out these de facto heroes to deliver us from crises. It was only after several years of working with both the vaunted and their more humbly-titled brethren that we came to an interesting realization: A-listers were successful not because they had superior programming skills, but because they took the time to learn why they were building the software in the first place. They sought clarity from the onset, gathering vital information and incorporating it into their design. If the pertinent information wasn't readily available, they used deductive reasoning to devise a plan to obtain it. Once they found clarity, they had the freedom to innovate and the ability to outperform their colleagues.

When we recognized that the real superpower at play here was the foresight to seek out hidden clarity, we introduced a visual control—a kanban—to provide clarity to the entire team. It wasn't long before we discovered B- and C-list coders rose to meet or even surpass their A-list colleagues. The logical conclusion here: A-list artistry is not born of technical prowess, but of clarity of purpose.[1]

---

1   Heroes are still necessary, so long as your system does not create false needs for them. With a tendency to seek out clarity, the hero's "talent" is best applied to those areas where information is at a minimum, like R&D or seeking out opportunities for kaizen.

CLARITY CONQUERS ALL

Existential Overhead:

- » Existential overhead impedes effectiveness.
- » Clarity dispels existential overhead.

Manufactured Emergencies:

- » Routinely responding to emergencies begets more emergencies.
- » Clarity leads to kaizen, which breaks the cycle of emergencies.

Knowledge Deficit:

- » We can't act on information we don't have.
- » Clarity creates—and is created by—actionable, meaningful information.

Hero Worship:

- » Reliance on heroes undermines daily operations.
- » Clarity raises the bar for "normal" workers.

When we have clarity, we use our time efficiently, we act with informed certainty, and we do a better job. Regardless of hero or non-hero status, even if the project itself is not a success, everyone can excel with clarity, everyone can provide value.

LIMIT YOUR WORK-IN-PROGRESS

Psychologist Abraham Maslow's oft-quoted and perpetually misunderstood "Hierarchy of Needs" depicts interdependent levels of human physical, social, and psychological need. Clarity is not an esoteric luxury, it is universally essential. So why then, among a list of the instinctive needs of a fully functioning person, is clarity nowhere to be found?

Did Maslow forget? Absolutely not.

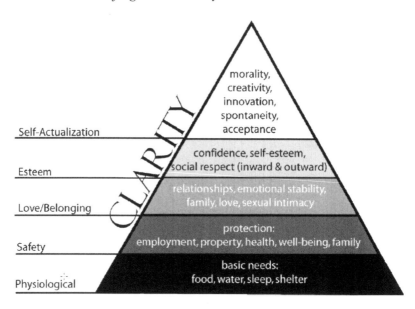

Clarity is a transcendent property, and an integral component of everything from shelter to self-actualization. Without clarity, it would be difficult to fully realize any of the elements within Maslow's hierarchy.

Let's talk about shelter, one of the most basic human needs and one many of us take for granted. Simply obtaining a place to stay doesn't necessarily satisfy that need. Say your house has been destroyed by a flash flood and your insurance doesn't cover acts-of-god. Where yesterday stood a safe and beautiful home, all you have left today is rubble and mortgage payments. A benevolent neighbor might open his home to you. For the moment, technically you have shelter. But that shelter isn't really yours and so you are filled with questions. *How long will I be welcome here? Is my safety assured? Whose rules must I follow? Where will I go if I get kicked out?* With this much ambiguity, is the need really being met?

A need is only truly met—that level of Maslow's hierarchy completely satisfied—when there is clarity around it. In this case, the need for shelter is fulfilled only if there is a sense of stability around it, when there is an assurance it won't be taken away.

Many of us fear growth, being pressured to change in some areas before other more basic needs have been met. When a need is secured we're better equipped to explore additional needs. We begin to shed our fears of growth and change by building on the security of already-won needs.

This doesn't mean we have to fulfill them in order— Maslow's hierarchy is not a linear to-do list. You can lack shelter but still have confidence, for example. It does mean that as you gain courage through satisfying some needs, it becomes easier to satisfy new ones on your path to self-actualization.

▶ **Neurotic anxiety is a symptom of the fact that some previous crisis has not been met, and to remove the symptom without helping the person get at his underlying conflict is to rob him of his best direction-finder and motivation for self understanding and growth. ~Rollo May[2]**

According to May and Maslow, we progress towards actualization when we adopt a mindset that minimizes fear and embraces growth.[3] For many of us, accepting shelter from a neighbor is not sustainable. Fears about the loss of the shelter need (e.g. "Whose rules must I follow") are rational and understandable. These fears can be overwhelming.

Ruled by fear, obsession takes hold. We act on the fear of losing the shelter rather than work on finding more permanent housing. Fear drives us to hold onto the temporary manifestation instead of reasoning out how to satisfy the need more sustainably.

In the absence of clarity, it's easy to become mired in fear. Personal Kanban visualizes and demystifies our fears, transforming them into issues to solve and tasks to take action on.

Recognizing our work's context and understanding its ramifications gives us clarity. We're able to move from a mindset dominated by existential overhead to one sensitized to kaizen. When we visualize our work, we can focus. In this context, "focus" doesn't mean locking our office door, selecting a task to process, and tuning out the world around us until that task is complete. That kind of

---

2   *Rollo May, Psychology and the Human Dilemma (New York: Norton, 1967) p. 82.*
3   *Abraham H. Maslow, Toward a Psychology of Being (New York: Van Nostrand Rheinhold, 1968).*

self-exile is a productivity (fear) reaction—not a kaizen (growth) reaction—to a stressful workload.

A kaizen reaction analyzes a situation, ascertains the level of clarity, and seeks out the most efficient paths to completion / innovation / additional clarity. Some days that might, in fact, require hiding in your office and blasting through a series of tasks until they're complete. Other days it might require slowing down, conducting some research or finding someone with whom to share the workload. Our personal growth and a quality product both require clarity.

▶ **I can see clearly now, the rain is gone. I can see all obstacles in my way. ~ Johnny Nash**

By providing transparency into the people, activities, and responsibilities guiding our daily lives, Personal Kanban promotes clarity of purpose. We see what we've promised and to whom we've promised it. We see environmental and emotional factors as they shift. We can assess how our plans and priorities will have to adapt in response to those changes. Clarity allows us to focus more, plan better, and find our rhythm, helping us strike a balance between the forces of push and pull.

▶ **Genius is personal, decided by fate, but it expresses itself by means of system. There is no work of art without system. ~ Le Corbusier**

Facilitating the completion of quality work, Personal Kanban bolsters our self-esteem. Rooted in the self-actualization level of Maslow's hierarchy, it provides a tool (a "system," as Le Corbusier explains) to recognize patterns and spontaneously solve problems. By visualizing our work and limiting its flow, the value of our options becomes apparent. The choices we make and actions we pursue have a much greater chance of reflecting our ethics, our aesthetics, and our dreams—components intrinsic to a balanced life.

COURSE CORRECTIONS: THE REALITY OF REPRIORITIZATION

Imagine a container of metal hurtling through space, heading towards Pluto. Now consider how for an astral body, Pluto is a tad eccentric. One day it's a bona fide planet and the next day, not so much. It doesn't orbit the sun in a circle, but instead travels in an elongated ellipse. Some days it's 2.65 billion kilometers from Earth, while other days it can be as far away as 4.68 billion—that's a 2 billion kilometer variation.[4]

Suffice it to say, Pluto is a difficult target.

NASA has never been an organization to shy away from a challenge, and so in 2006 it launched the New Horizons robotic spacecraft. This half ton unmanned rocket is scheduled to fly by Pluto on July 14, 2015. Given that it will take nearly a decade between launch and final con-

---

4   *Earth is only about 150 million kilometers from the Sun, so just the variation in distance between Earth and Pluto is about 13 times the distance between you and the Sun.*

twitter   Home Profile Find People Settings He

Tracking says we need a small course
correction burn next year. Just 0.5
meters/sec (1 mile/hr) but without,
we'd miss Pluto by ~80,000 km.

 NewHorizons2015

tact, members of the New Horizons mission have to be
fairly patient to see the return on their work.

Despite traveling at near-record speed, Pluto is still a long
way off. In order for the probe to reach its destination,
a mid-flight correction of about one mile per hour was
necessary. While this correction seems small (it would
be nearly impossible to replicate in your car), it is in no
way insignificant. Seemingly minor tweaks translate into
major results.

The craft is propelled by some rocket fuel and a whole
lot of time and money. Imagine if you were a member of
the launch team and after waiting almost a decade you
missed your target by 80,000 kilometers. That's half the
distance between Earth and the Sun. *Talk about a bad day
at the office!*

Considering the size of the mission, the cost of change is
relatively low: a routine course correction of 1/36,000th
of the craft's speed. The cost of failure, on the other hand,
is exceedingly high: $650 million. Making course cor-
rections while they're still small ensures success with the
least degree of disruption.

Often we assume written plans are etched in stone, and so we feel compelled to adhere to them at any and all costs. But no matter how well-thought out or well-funded they may be, projects are seldom precise. Some deviation from the original plan is inevitable and frequent small adjustments are unavoidable.

Without realizing it, we instinctively course correct all the time. Take driving, for example. If I told you to drive down a straight road for two hours only touching the steering wheel every half hour, would you consider it?

Not without airbags.

Yet we still feel we're in control of our car, even though we make minute course corrections every second. It's this ability to be flexible, to adjust to changes in our context, that allow us to be successful.

Course corrections are not project management failures, nor do they suggest a loss of control—quite the opposite in fact. Rigid plans with fixed definitions of success limit our options and invite failure. Whether it's planning Carl's daughter's education or an interplanetary mission, adjustments are natural and necessary.

Structure misleading implies security. Well-laid plans make us feel safe. Once we define the path towards an objective, we somehow feel our future is ensured. For many of us, rigorous up-front planning is ingrained in our psyche, so much so that anything else feels uncertain, less scientific, like we're operating without a net. Blindly followed plans are no substitute for being attentive, and adjusting our actions to best serve our goals.

Predicated on observation, experimentation, and adjustment, Personal Kanban is much more reliable and scientific than mere guesswork. Now that we've allowed ourselves the freedom to adapt to our surroundings, it's time to acknowledge our emotions and intentions.

THE BEDROCK OF INTROSPECTION

▶ **What good is experience if you do not reflect? ~ Fredrick the Great**

It's noon and you're famished. There's a pizzeria, a hamburger joint, and a taco truck nearby, but your doctor wants you to watch your weight and you know you're best served by grabbing a made-to-order salad at Uncle Phil's organic market instead. As luck would have it, Uncle Phil's is 20 minutes away, and your next meeting is in an hour. You could drive there and—barring any traffic or a line at the express check out—take 20 minutes to order and quickly eat, and another 20 minutes to drive back to work. To play it safe you could reschedule your meeting, or you could just grab some fast food and make up for those extra calories at dinner.

Are these decisions as monumental as reorienting a multi-million dollar spacecraft? Maybe, maybe not. But every choice involves a decision between one option or course of action over its alternatives, and every choice impacts another. Deciding on Uncle Phil's may force you to move out that meeting one-half hour, which will then delay an afternoon appointment. So whether we realize it or not, we engage in reprioritization—the cognitive process of options trading—all day long.

Do we trade our options with a long-term pragmatic view, a short-term emotional one, or a combination of the two? Is the decision to stick to a healthy diet a pragmatic one, or an emotional one? And what about the decision to keep a meeting as scheduled to get product out the door on time?

At the moment we make them, pragmatic decisions and emotional decisions are often indistinguishable. We need to revisit our decisions after the fact, because while we may know the outcome, do we really understand the motivation? It takes a healthy dose of Monday morning quarterbacking to examine and evaluate our mental processes to fully understand what it is that drives us.

That's where introspection comes in. When we're introspective, we observe our thought processes to understand the reasoning behind our decisions. We look at past events through the filter of our own emotions, motivations, and biases. *Why did we decide on A over B? Whose interests were we really serving? Did we make the best choice? Did our choice make us happy?* This is the point where we give ourselves the information we need to make good decisions in the future.

A truly pragmatic decision balances facts, external forces, desires, and a host of other situational factors. This balance can only be achieved through introspection. With introspection, we come to understand whether our priorities truly balance our needs and our emotions.

RETROSPECTIVES

▶ **If you want to know your past, look into your present conditions. If you want to know your future, look into your present actions. ~ Buddhist Saying**

▶ **May you have the hindsight to know where you've been, the foresight to know where you are going, and the insight to know when you have gone too far. ~ Irish Saying**

but

▶ **Past performance is no guarantee of future returns. ~ Wall Street Saying**

Yesterday's lessons inform tomorrow's promise, or so countless motivational quotes tell us. Nevertheless, those who stand the most to gain from predicting the future—Wall Street traders—are painfully aware that what worked in the past is not necessarily repeatable.

Once again, variation presents itself.

The experience we gain from past successes and failures gives us insight into what we want to replicate and what we want to avoid going forward. We want to focus on *the context* that led to success or to failure—not necessarily the success or failure itself. Looking back on the context of our work through retrospectives adds another dimension to Personal Kanban.[5]

Retrospectives are regular and ritualized moments of collective reflection. A practice common to the Agile and

---

5   *This is also why Personal Kanban only has two rules. Rigid systems invite failure. Flexible systems invite customization. Always strive to have as few rules and as few controls as possible.*

Lean communities, retrospectives allow a team to pause and consider what went well with their project, what didn't go as expected, and what could be improved going forward.

Regular retrospectives enable us to identify and act on opportunities for positive change. Whether we hold them on our own, with our families, or with our team at work, retrospectives are an essential tool for reflection.

Retrospectives can take place at whatever intervals you're comfortable with, and—keeping in mind the more frequent, the fresher things are in your mind—for whatever duration you choose. These exercises give individuals as well as teams the opportunity to recognize accomplishments (celebration), bemoan setbacks (catharsis), and re-orient a project for future action (kaizen event). Retrospectives demonstrate that whether or not things went well in the past, there's always room for kaizen to innovate in the service of increased effectiveness. When retrospectives occur on a consistent schedule, they allow for small low-cost / high-return course corrections.

It's helpful to feature a **RETROSPECTIVE** column as the final column of your Personal Kanban. As tasks are cleared from **DONE**, put them in the **RETROSPECTIVE** column. At the beginning or end of each week hold a retrospective and quickly examine completed tasks. Acknowledge what went well and what could be improved next time. Celebrate victories. Learn from defeats.

You don't have to wait to hold a retrospective. Especially in those situations where a task or project has been derailed, gather the appropriate people together to examine the problem and use it as a learning opportunity. Emergency retrospectives allow the individuals involved to team up on the problem and devise a solution.

Years ago I contracted with a company to have two windows installed in the corner of my bathroom, explaining the area around the tub needed more light and ventilation. When the installation was complete, I was shocked to discover that the windows did not open. I assumed that by explaining I wanted the windows for ventilation, having them actually open would be a given.

This was at the height of the housing boom, so if I upset my contractor I feared I would end up with holes in my walls for months on end until I could find someone else to complete the job. I needed to be tactful. The contractor and I held a quick retrospective. I assigned no blame but instead focused on getting the windows replaced with ones that actually opened. We agreed that in the future when changes were made, we'd be more specific about expectations. The "misunderstanding" with the windows required an immediate retrospective because it was an identifiable, "stop the line" kind of problem.[6] Whether you're working alone, with your family, or with a team, don't pass up opportunities to address issues before they escalate.

Just as your Personal Kanban can assume myriad forms, a retrospective can also take the shape of whatever works within your current context. Whether you're just finish-

---

6   A concept integral to Lean manufacturing, any team member is empowered to stop the assembly line if they notice a critical issue requires immediate attention or assistance from their co-workers. The principle here is that fixing a problem when it arises—even if it interrupts the flow of work—saves time and money in the long run.

ing a weekend project in the garage, or on day fourteen of hurricane disaster relief, taking a few moments to check your processes and ensure any issues are corrected will help you improve what you're currently doing, or the way you go about doing it in the future.

Remember, you don't have to be mid-flight to Pluto to gain from minor course corrections. You want to pilot your work as attentively as you drive your car. As with driving, your fine-tuning and retrospectives will become a natural part of working. When you master the art of the retrospective, you are honing in on kaizen.

SOLVING PROBLEMS AT THEIR SOURCE

▶ **The root cause of any problem is the key to a lasting solution. ~ Taiichi Ohno**

Despite our best efforts, life doesn't always go according to plan. When things go wrong, our first line of defense is to identify who or what appears to be responsible. We want the problem to go away and, anxious for resolution, we barely scratch the issue's surface before assigning blame. We feel better. We consider the issue closed. We move on.

For the record, this is a lousy approach to problem solving. Not only is it superficial and short-sighted, it's a missed opportunity to improve and benefit from a kaizen event. By visualizing our work and understanding its flow, we can solve problems at their source.

The following trouble shooting techniques delve deep into the heart of a problem, challenging conventional wisdom, getting rid of wasteful assumptions, and exposing root causes.

Pattern Matching as a Foundation for Problem Solving

▶ **The human brain finds it incredibly difficult, if not impossible, to fake randomness. ~ Alex Bellosh**

Pattern recognition. It's been hard-wired into our brains since we were warding off sabre-toothed tigers. Drawing connections between related objects and behaviors, humans have an innate ability to seek, draw relationships between, and store patterns. Inferring and adapting to basic differences in nature—such as distinguishing between animals that were potentially harmful or plants that were toxic or the amount of sunlight relative to each season—was key to prehistoric man's survival and our evolution as a species.

Synthesizing patterns—connecting the dots, so to speak—allows us to interpret and make assumptions about our environment. By the age of three months, we already perceive and act on patterns. We start with the simple: recognizing the tone of our mother's voice then moving to the texture of our favorite stuffed bear. With time we begin to make inferences from more complex patterns, like guessing our supervisor's reaction after we've submitted our expense report late for three consecutive months.

LIMIT YOUR WORK-IN-PROGRESS

Personal Kanban takes advantage of this most basic trait. Visualizing tasks and engaging with them physically and cognitively allows us to comprehend patterns in our work. We see which tasks have the quickest throughput, which tend to become blocked, which generally require no assistance whatsoever.

With time, we become sensitized to existing and emerging patterns. We learn that small changes are less taxing and—because they don't engage the brain's fear response—are more successful than larger ones. Sensitization is a powerful tool, and so the more that you look for an opportunity to improve, the more likely it is that you will find one.

Opportunities for improvement usually arise when a change in pattern is detected, when something presents itself as problematic. Poorly performing patterns are often merely symptoms of an underlying problem. Addressing symptoms may ease the pain, but it does little to ensure sustainability. For that we need to expose the problem's root cause. This can be done using simple yet robust techniques called "root cause analyses." While there are a great many to choose from, we suggest beginning with two of the simplest: The Five Whys and the Socratic Method.

The Five Whys

Tonianne and I have similar stories, tales of our younger selves greatly testing our respective fathers' patience with an exchange that went something like this:

Dad Benson/DeMaria: *You have an excuse for everything!*

Jim/Toni: *No, I have a reason for everything.*

Not one of the four of us ever explored the root cause of our debate. So rather than these exchanges becoming an opportunity for growth, they remained little more than inert banter between two smart-mouthed kids and their frustrated dads. They could have proven our reasons were excuses. We could have proven our excuses were reasons. In the end, these differences in agreement were lost opportunities for all involved.

Japanese industrialist and founder of Toyota Industries Sakichi Toyoda understood that problems often have nested causes. He wanted people to get past their preconceptions and "with a blank mind" get to the heart of the issue.[7] He didn't ask *Why?* once, or even twice. Repeat 'why' five times to every matter, he instructed, until you arrive at something with real context.

To see the Five Whys in action, consider the following scenario: You return home late from work one night to discover your kitchen counter teeming with ants, a sink full of dirty dishes, and your teenage son Billy nowhere

---

7 *Jeffrey Liker, The Toyota Way (New York: McGraw Hill, 2003) p. 223.*

to be found. It was Billy's turn to do the dishes, and since Billy is MIA, you turn to your daughter for answers:

1. *Why weren't the dishes cleaned?* Because Billy didn't wash them. (Blame!)

2. *Why?* Because he wasn't in the kitchen. (Negligence!)

3. *Why?* Because he was in his bedroom all day. (Gross Negligence!)

4. *Why?* Because he was studying. (Um...)

5. *Why?* Because he is taking the SAT tomorrow. (Well, okay. That makes sense)

Stopping after the first *Why?* confuses the symptom with the cause, and has the potential to get Billy into all sorts of unwarranted trouble. Drilling down to the heart of the matter exposes an actionable reason for the event. In this case, Billy didn't wash the dishes because of demonstrably good prioritization. Like Personal Kanban, the Five Whys depersonalizes a problem. No longer does the conversation begin and end with blaming Billy. Instead, you're driven to ask a more accurate and constructive question: *Why didn't Billy **tell** someone that he couldn't wash the dishes?*

The bugs are still an issue, and Billy will probably have to kick in some of his allowance to pay for pest control. But applying the Five Whys produces enough hard data to disprove original assumptions about the problem's cause, demonstrating instead that the infestation resulted from a communication breakdown, and not your teenager's questionable work ethic.

We see that Five Whys beat one knee-jerk reaction.

Working to find a root cause respects Billy's ability to make a decision. The root cause analysis determines he needs to be better about checking in, which is fairly easy to accommodate. Ultimately this discovery—that there's a better way to communicate with family—generates a kaizen event, a moment of inspiration that leads to an improvement. Improvement here has the potential to save the family from future problems, whereas simple punishment does not.

Note: When it comes to administering the Five Whys, five is a good start, but an arbitrary number nonetheless. You can go deeper or less so as your situation dictates. Stopping at five probably isn't rigorous enough for solving the U.S. health care crisis, for example. Let the exploration of root causes be your goal. Don't obsess over the number of "whys" you employ.

Socratic Method

▶ **I know you won't believe me, but the highest form of human excellence is to question oneself and others. ~ Socrates**

While you can't give someone an epiphany, you can help them reach one on their own.

Socrates did just this. The philosopher engaged his students in an intellectual exchange where assumptions were challenged, hypotheses were eliminated, and understanding was pursued through a generative process of inquiry.

The Socratic Method is meant to go deep, quite deep in fact, and so it would be a little wordy to script out the process like we did the Five Whys (five is a mercifully small number). Instead, we're left to imagine how Socrates would apply his dialectic magic to a familiar problem...

Baffled by the argument you just had with your wife, you need some space. You and Socrates head to the doughnut shop where you lament *What the hell just happened? Why did we just have that breakdown?* Between bites of his honey-glazed kruller, Socrates asks you a series of questions designed to make you redefine "breakdown," and perhaps even "we," recognizing that all along you've endowed these words with a host of assumptions.

Without giving it much thought, you contend the breakdown began at the point in your conversation where you became upset. But "when you got upset" is simply an abstraction, and gives you nothing actionable to address. As Socrates calmly begins to question your definitions, the exact point of the breakdown begins to shift from when you got upset to when your spouse hit a trigger— those words she used that caused you to get upset. As he continues questioning, the breakdown moves back to the point where you started the conversation. Soon you find that "breakdown" is not a point in time at all, but a byproduct of an action that upset you. Then, after four cups of coffee, you have an epiphany: *Arguments like that are the product of a number of colliding bits of stress, fear, and existential overhead!* You wave your arms excitedly because you now have clarity, and the problem that seemed inexplicable just a few hours ago is suddenly demystified.

Since Socrates knew this all along, he could have summed up your breakdown with a dismissive *Dude, it's just a byproduct of how you guys treat each other.* But he would have understated the situation and overstated the problem. You didn't need his opinion, you needed an epiphany—a eureka moment where a life-changing realization is made.

Socrates' longer process of inquiry helped you eliminate wasteful assumptions and arrive at your own conclusion; having created it, you now own it. Remember that Confucius quote, "Tell me and I forget. Show me and I remember. Let me do and I understand." The Socratic method entails doing to foster understanding.

Socrates is often compared to a midwife. Of course he wasn't helping deliver babies, he helped birth intellect. To Socrates, knowledge was not something to be gained passively, but instead was something to be pursued in an interactive exercise.

In the self-application of the Socratic Method, you question your own assumptions, stripping away confounding information to reveal the truth embedded in your position. Critical self-inquiry—playing your own devil's advocate—requires both patience and honesty, but is essential in the quest for improvement. As Socrates shows us, so many of the assumptions we operate under are intellectual waste. They cause us to react to symptoms, blame prematurely, and stop before we ever reach a solution.

LIMIT YOUR WORK-IN-PROGRESS

Reality Check

In the hands of a novice, the Five Whys and the Socratic Method can be blunt instruments used to browbeat rather than problem-solve. Rigorous leading questions put people on the defensive, quickly turning a constructive dialogue into an adversarial debate. Successful application of these methods requires finesse, so be sure to use them in a constructive way to solve a problem collaboratively, rather than in a destructive way that hones in on failure.

PKFLOW TIPS

1. Heroes are often misapplied.

2. Clarity is the cornerstone of growth.

3. Growth requires retrospection and introspection.

4. Course corrections are necessary in any endeavor.

5. Retrospectives give us the time to balance long and short term needs.

6. Solve problems at their source, don't be fooled by the obvious answer.

ENDGAME

Visualize Your Work
Limit Your Work-in-Progress

The game of Personal Kanban has a grand goal: to live effectively. To win at this game, we need to define our work, rather than let our work define us. To escape the tyranny of push, we must complete what we start, exercise options for effectiveness, and increase the occurrence of what brings us joy. To achieve these objectives, we need to understand both our work and our relationship to it. A wonderful, circular and self-perpetuating system, Personal Kanban creates a narrative map of our past, present, and future actions in which to identify patterns and innovate. In the end, Personal Kanban enables us to reduce fear and make better choices.

The challenge is to make sure that when we exercise an option—when we dynamically reprioritize—we understand the emotions at play. We see the choices we're making. We see our fear, we see our desires. Our choices become tangible and therefore harder to ignore. We will always value some choices while resenting others, that's just human. Our goal here is not to stifle emotion, but to understand where and when it acts as our enemy or ally.

Infomercial hyperbole would sum up with: *PERSONAL KANBAN HELPS YOU DO MORE WITH LESS.* We don't want to simply do *more*. We want to do *right*. We want to do *better*. We want to choose tasks that, over time, increase our options, encourage experimentation, and lead to balanced and successful lives.

To exercise the right options we need to understand context. When we complete one task and are deciding which to pull next, we ask ourselves a lot of the "right" questions, logical ones like *What's most important? Which will fit in the amount of time I have? Which helps me in the long run? Which is most important to others I care about?*

But…

Certain situations elicit strong emotional and physiological reactions. We tell ourselves *I hate doing that, so I'm not going to,* or *That task depresses me and I'm going to watch television,* or *I'll do that later…much, much later.* But we want to be effective and therefore procrastination makes us anxious. We become apprehensive, irritable, and angry. While we don't often acknowledge the legitimacy of these most basic and primitive responses, they deserve our recognition nonetheless, as they contain authentic and invaluable feedback about the way particular circumstances make us feel.

Our emotions come from a murky, complicated place inhabited by our memories, our insecurities, and our projections for the future. We're afraid to take on challenges because either success or failure will take us into the unknown. Sometimes it's our preferences—we simply don't *like* doing whatever it is that we need to do. Sometimes it's fears we harbor from the past—ghosts telling us we failed before and will fail again. Sometimes it's defeatism—recognition that we're not very good at a particular task and we don't relish the thought of doing a poor job. These fears stunt our growth.

We generate our own emergencies by overextending ourselves and then addressing those tasks only when they become dire. Visualizing our work helps us appropriately channel our efforts by not letting us hide unattractive tasks in the recesses of our minds. Without visualization, prioritization is reactionary and thoughtless. Our actions gravitate towards the emergency du jour. We repeat this fatalistic and self-defeating process until soon everything presents itself as urgent. After a while, we begin to assume that this is just the nature of life.

To answer the question posed in Chapter 1: *No, This is not as good as it gets.* **Life is much more.**

Personal Kanban depersonalizes and demystifies our work. It aligns our emotions with our goals, and transforms our fears from a specter to a sticky note. Visualization gives us the information we need into understand how we prioritize and respond to real or imagined emergencies. It allows us to schedule for completion, giving us the flexibility to correct on-the-fly. Tasks can be prioritized based on context. Risk assessments can be conducted with confidence. Sure, there will be times when we misjudge, but overall our decisions will be better informed.

Personal Kanban helps us find what we truly enjoy and excel at so we can optimize our time and attention to suit.

~

If there are two takeaways from this book, we hope they are: *Work unseen is work uncontrolled* and *We can't (and shouldn't!) do more work than we can handle.*

We've learned how we react cognitively and emotionally to maps, narratives, and clarity. We've learned that large upfront planning is wasteful and destroys options. We've learned that context drives our decisions. We've learned that retrospectives help us understand our ways of working, our passions, and our potential futures. We've learned that decisions made in the absence of clarity are decisions in peril. We've learned that life is complex and cannot be taken for granted.

We need to respect natural variation and we need to respect ourselves. Personal Kanban can help us see life's complexities and make better decisions. With introspection, kaizen, and retrospectives we are better informed, more attentive, and relaxed.

Personal Kanban is not a panacea—nothing is. It is our guide. Always changing and ever evolving, it is our map of living.

APPENDIX A
PERSONAL KANBAN
DESIGN PATTERNS

▶ **Results! Why, man, I have gotten a lot of results. I know several thousand things that won't work. ~ Thomas Edison**

Your Personal Kanban is your laboratory. You'll always be changing your conditions, introducing new data, validating or disproving hypotheses, and innovating. Experimenting with your Personal Kanban is not only acceptable, it's encouraged. Just be sure to keep limiting your WIP.

In Chapter 1, you were introduced to a basic Personal Kanban. As with any tool, consistent use begets proficiency, often creating the need for an "upgrade." With a clear understanding of your context and a little creativity, there are endless ways to visualize, interact with, and learn from your work.

In this section we provide a series of design patterns—alternative Personal Kanban visualizations that approach the challenges of tracking work from different angles.

Again, there is no right or wrong way to create your Personal Kanban. You are constrained only by your imagination and the materials at your disposal. Configure it in circles, add additional columns or value streams, construct it using magnets or velcro or Lego, even. Don't be afraid to take chances and create a visualization that might not work out. In the end, trial and error is the basis for learning what works best for you.

JESSICA'S STORY: FUTURE IN PROGRESS AND MULTIPLE VALUE STREAMS

Jessica is a single mom, and a busy one at that. She juggles two jobs, each located on opposite ends of her city. She's studying for her financial advisor certification. She's training for a triathlon. She wants to write a book. She's thinking about opening her own business, perhaps getting another degree. The list goes on.

As a mathematician and an expert in intangible assets, Jessica understands she has so much on her plate that busting her WIP limit is almost guaranteed, and money is just one asset to focus on out of many.

One Sunday over brunch, we mapped out her Personal Kanban. We discussed what she enjoyed, what she valued, what her aspirations were. Within minutes of what would become a three hour conversation, it became apparent that Jessica was not simply goal-oriented, she was a goal-collector. First and foremost, we needed to get that under control. Setting well-defined and achievable goals is admirable, but when they generate more tasks than we can handle they need to be tamed.

We agreed she needed more than a WIP limit, she needed a "Future in Progress" or *FIP* limit. With the certification, the triathlon, the book she wants to write etc., it made sense to choose two of these goals and, no pun intended, run with them. The certification was immediately necessary for her job and her short-term financial needs, so she couldn't say no to that. The triathlon motivated her to exercise regularly and maintain a healthy lifestyle, so that too was an obvious choice. As for her other goals, she could explore them later but for now, Jessica had more of an opportunity to succeed with a FIP limit of two.

That was step one.

Step two entailed visualizing her FIP alongside her regular WIP. Jessica's triathlon regimen included both repetitive and non-repetitive tasks. On a daily basis she needed to consume a specific number of calories, take her vitamins, and of course work out, swim, bike, or run. This could equate to three repetitive, overhead-contributing sticky notes per day, every day. She also needed to maintain a rigorous study schedule while making time for the other obligations in her life.

So many tickets, too little real information. Personal Kanban is about quality, not quantity. Effectiveness, not productivity. Tasks that provide value, not simply generate inventory.

Personal Kanban is built to be an information radiator. Like the gauges in her Honda, Jessica's Personal Kanban had to give her real-time, actionable information like:

» Which workouts did she complete and on which days?

» What was her endurance level like during her workout?

» In which activity is her competitive time strongest?

» In which activity is her performance weakest?

» How did she feel afterwards?

» Did her caloric intake match her workouts?

» What days was she able to focus on studying?

» Which modules are her strongest?

» Which material is she least comfortable with?

Armed with this information, Jessica can see where her workouts excel and where they fall short. She can see where her training time and her study time conflict. She can monitor the impact her workouts have on other aspects of her life. She can note imbalances between work and family. She can make course corrections as needed.

Jessica's whiteboard was small, so we worked with the surrounding wall to make up for lost real estate (both her **BACKLOG** and **DONE** columns exist off the board). Her spontaneous tasks are color-coded by type, and flow through a **TODAY -> DOING -> DONE** value stream. But that's not the defining feature here.

Her Personal Kanban includes two additional "swim lanes." A swim lane is an additional value stream or horizontal lane dedicated to specific tasks. The first swim lane is dedicated to Triathlon Training. We had several metrics here:

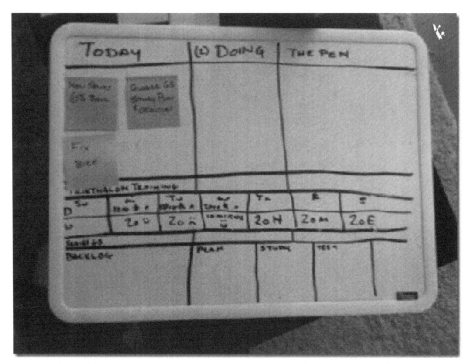

Diet: Each day net calorie consumption, hydration, and vitamin intake are tracked; calories are assigned a number, water and vitamins are each given a check mark to signify the daily requirement has been met.

Workout: Type, severity, and subjective well being (SWB) are all noted here. The "20" represents 20 minutes of cardio. Letters E, M, H represent easy, medium, and hard workouts. Happy or sad faces measure how Jessica subjectively felt about the workout.

Not only do these metrics reflect Jessica's dedication and progress, they also serve as a baseline for planning subsequent workouts.

The second swim lane is dedicated to Certification Prep. Jessica's preferred method of learning entails setting up a study guide for each module, reviewing the material, then taking practice quizzes. So we created a swim lane with a WIP limit of one to ensure that at any point, she could only be working on one module.

Jessica's board incorporates two approaches: the Sequestering Approach addresses repetitive tasks, while the Large Project Approach visualizes value streams for specific projects. Let's explore each in more detail.

SEQUESTERING APPROACH: DEALING WITH REPETITIVE TASKS

Jessica's pre-race regimen requires her to track her performance, nutrition, and body metrics. Had she created a single, all-encompassing task entitled "Train for Triathlon," crucial daily requirements risked becoming over-shadowed by (non FIP-related) tasks that in the short term appeared more pressing. The Sequestering Approach is specifically designed to deal with repetitive tasks in an elegant way. When they're incorporated into your regular WIP limit, repetitive tasks can clutter your Personal Kanban and create wasteful overhead. If you have to check in with three customers daily, creating fifteen sticky notes per week reminding you to contact them is waste. In these types of situations, consider giving repetitive tasks their own visualization and WIP treatment. Sequester them in a dedicated area of your Personal Kanban. When a task is complete, simply check that day's box.

It is important to keep these tasks visible, even if they've become a habit. They still constitute WIP, and their impact on other work should be acknowledged.

LARGE PROJECT APPROACH

Sometimes we're faced with large projects like Jessica's triathlon and certification prep that anticipate months of work and encompass a host of associated tasks. Projects like these require their own distinct value stream to track their progress and flow independent of other tasks. Here's why.

Say you're writing a book. Having a single "Work on Book" sticky note sitting in **DOING** for months on end doesn't acknowledge the project's flow: it doesn't show book progress, chapter progress, where or why you got hung up, and if your work reveals any recurring patterns. Ideally, you want to track progress made on each chapter through the pre-writing, writing, editing, and finalization stages.

Adding separate, dedicated swim lanes to your Personal Kanban helps you visualize related tasks. This approach continues to let you manage your overall WIP while giv-

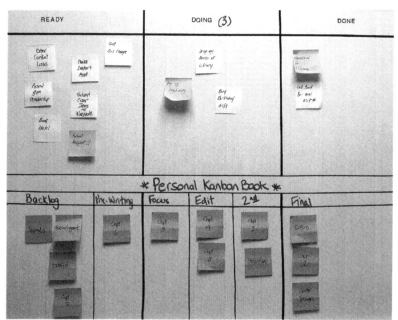

ing you control over and insight into the flow of your projects.

The Large Project Approach is two-phased. First, it visualizes the project in a "roll up" task which consolidates the project into a single sticky note. In the image, the roll up task is represented by the first dark sticky note in **DOING**. "Work on Book" resides in your WIP, and serves as a proxy for all those individual tasks related to the book writing project. It then tracks the book's progress through its own distinct value stream (the secondary or lower value stream in the image). In this particular project, chapters move from one stage to the next until the book is complete, but you can have individual tasks or other objects of value represented, so long as the work is visualized.

EMERGENCY RESPONSE APPROACH: TAMING UNEXPECTED WORKLOADS

With life comes emergencies, and with emergencies come tasks. Ones we never asked for. Ones we're not prepared for.

Ones that don't respect our pull system.

When I was a teenager, a series of seven tornadoes ripped apart Grand Island, Nebraska. The June 3rd tornados killed five, injured hundreds, and obliterated my home town. Its devastation was so profound, Hollywood made an (equally horrific) TV movie out of it. The morning after that historic "night of the twisters," bewildered yet determined residents in our community of 30,000 had a WIP-busting set of tasks confronting them.

Now this was an emergency with a capital "E," and so no one had the luxury of slack. People had to find temporary housing, salvage what they could from the wreckage, arrange for insurance adjusters, raze what little remained of their homes, create reconstruction plans, and rebuild their lives. And they had to accomplish all of this without electricity, telephones, or running water, during a week of 90 degree temps and oppressive humidity.

From a roof overhead to existential overhead.

An Emergency Response Personal Kanban could have helped them deal with the aftermath. Imagine climbing out of your basement at dawn on June 4th to discover that from the ground floor up your home was gone. Suddenly you're faced with a barrage of unexpected and time-sensitive tasks (like finding shelter). For many tasks, resolution requires external input. If you worked through them serially, within the confines of a WIP limit, most of your time would be spent waiting for your calls to be returned, your claims to be processed, or your materials to be delivered. In an emergency response situation, you simply don't have time to fully complete each task before starting a new one, and tracking individual sub-tasks such as "Check on insurance paperwork AGAIN" is a waste of your time.

If you were to use a standard Personal Kanban, you'd have a problem. Tasks begun but not yet completed would either clog up your WIP or clutter your **PEN**. But this project is self-contained, meaning it is highly directed and focused, necessitating the management of multiple tasks at once.

This is multitasking by necessity, but it's *controlled* multitasking. With a to-do list, we'd have an accounting of the tasks, but we wouldn't understand their state or be able to limit our WIP. The Emergency Response Approach includes a few helpful features that are designed to overcome the limitations of a to-do list.

For each task, the value stream for the Emergency Response Approach shows:

» **BEGUN** If it's been started (you've begun to work on the task).

Task	Begun	Assembling	Assembled	Active	Complete	Notes
Cancel utilities						
Sort wreckage						
get storage unit						
remove debris						
Schedule removal						
get temporary housing						
rent car						
buy clothes						
find contractor						
get new prescriptions from doc						
get spare glasses from doc						
get post office box						
change all credit card #s: VISA 1 / VISA 2 / AMEX / MASTERCARD						
Check on schools						
Im billing for relatives						
Call FEMA Re: Assistance						
buy cooler						
get generator						

> » **ASSEMBLING** If it's being assembled (you're gathering paperwork or other requirements).

> » **ASSEMBLED** If it's been assembled (requirements are complete).

> » **ACTIVE** If it's being processed (if you're waiting for someone else to act).

> » **COMPLETE** If it's complete.

The Emergency Response Approach also features a **NOTES** column. Notes will likely fill your Emergency Personal Kanban. They are necessary. Don't fear functional clutter. Is it optimal? No, but neither is life. This is your war room—the one place where, no matter what is happening, you can observe and know what is going on.

TIME CAPSULE APPROACH

Over time, we invariably amass a lot of small tasks that are important but not urgent. These tasks may start out benign, but the longer we put them off the more likely they'll spiral into crises, derailing our plans, requiring emergency reprioritization. These seemingly insignificant tasks are waste-in-waiting. They are the five minute tasks you never got to that in the end cost you 30 minutes to apologize for not doing.

The Time Capsule Approach helps you get a handle on those pesky tasks. Look at your Personal Kanban, see all those little tasks? Pull them all off the board, go to your desk, and start doing them until they're done or your day is over. If you have eight hours of small tasks, consider this a learning opportunity. Move them across the desk through three stations. **READY -> DOING -> DONE.**

This is now a speed tasking exercise. Don't spend a lot of time prioritizing. You will most likely game the system by doing one or a combination of the following:

Sweat (out) the small stuff: There's an old wives' tale that maintains "sweating it out" is the best way to beat a fever. Sure, turning up the heat when an infection is already spiking your temperature is uncomfortable, but some people swear it's a surefire way to get rid of the toxins making you sick.

It is in this particular vein that we say *Go ahead, turn up the heat on your backlog and sweat (out) the small stuff.* Quickly process those five minute ankle-biters. The discomfort you experience is only temporary and in the end, a satisfying number of those tasks filling up your **DONE** column leaves you with a backlog that is healthy and relevant.

Launch all missiles: Simple tasks that require little more than sending out a quick email are easy to pull into **DOING**. For the Time Capsule Approach however, **DONE** is the goal. Having multiple active tasks is okay, so long as they are steadily moving towards completion.

Remember, this is a strategy for coping with clutter in your backlog. Personal tasks are unruly, and so a messy backlog is inevitable. If you find yourself de-cluttering more than once a month, then it's likely you are overcommitting yourself, making your tasks too granular, or not prioritizing well enough.

LIMIT YOUR WORK-IN-PROGRESS

BALANCED THROUGHPUT APPROACH

When I ran Gray Hill, I was the only morning person in the company. So I would give my day a rolling start by going into the office at 6:30, writing a blog post, answering email, or getting some quick tasks out of the way before the rest of the staff showed up around 8:00. Beginning my morning with a series of small, undaunting, even enjoyable tasks eased me gently into my day, while moving those things off my plate quickly each morning gave my day momentum.

Had I been using Personal Kanban back then, the Balanced Throughput Approach is how I would visualize that type of work. This approach prioritizes a number of those small, quickly processed tasks and addresses them first. Large, more involved tasks are then handled throughout the course of the day. The goal here is not to process quantity over quality, but to balance task size and task type and to ensure at least a minimum amount of each are done regularly—staving off their accumulation and preventing marathon sessions where you *sweat (out) the small stuff.*

To accomplish this, the Balanced Throughput Approach gives you a WIP limit of three small tasks to get done quickly, then a WIP limit of two larger tasks to do later.

Note: Don't move completed tasks off your Balanced Throughput Personal Kanban until the end of the day or until all five tasks (large and small) are complete. If you complete them and then immediately replace them with

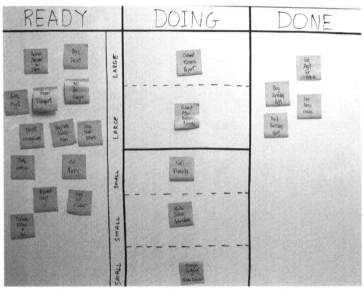

new tasks, you aren't actually balancing your throughput. This approach does not promote working simply for the sake of productivity. You aren't maximizing for throughput in the number of sticky notes you are moving, you are maximizing for throughput in different types of tasks.

PERSONAL KANBAN AND POMODORO

The Personal Kanban community has been quick to adopt the Pomodoro Technique when complete immersion is the only way to get a task out of WIP. The brainchild of Francesco Cirillo, this time management tool promotes focus using 25 minute increments for work, followed by five minutes of rest, repeating the process as needed.[1] During these bursts of intense concentration (tracked with the help of a kitchen timer, online clock, or anything with an alarm), tune out the distractions around you. Let that phone call roll over into voice mail, and that tepid cup of coffee will just have to wait to be reheated. This is the time for you to concentrate. Then, kick back and let your brain say *Ahhhhh*.

Pomodoro is a perfect complement to Personal Kanban, helping you process your WIP in 25 minute bursts. With Personal Kanban, you understand that you've organized your tasks, pulled the best one at the time, and will get to the others in due course. This makes it easier to focus and reach completion.

Note: Don't attempt to timebox all of your tasks in 25 minute intervals. To avoid burn out, use the Pomodoro Technique sparingly.

---

1   http://www.pomodorotechnique.com

PORTABLE PERSONAL KANBAN

Students, consultants, real estate brokers, fitness coaches, facilitators, teachers, district managers, parents. For those of us who don't spend the majority of our day in an office where a stationary Personal Kanban is always in sight, or for those times when we don't have access to our wall-mounted board, a portable Personal Kanban offers a functional alternative to visualize our work wherever we go.

Here we use a simple notebook and small sticky notes (a file folder works just as well). The top half of the page features the **READY** and **DOING** columns, while the lower half features the **DONE** column and **THE PEN**. This makes a simple and effective portable Personal Kanban that will let you not only manage your tasks on the go, but easily syncs up with your larger Personal Kanban at home or at the office.

APPENDIX B
PERSONAL KANBAN AND SOCIAL MEDIA

▶ **I have only two rules about this book. Learn to be more productive from this book. Talk about this book. ~ Ross Mayfield**

Personal Kanban may have been born of necessity, but the meme was bred in social media. Following that series of epiphanies we discussed in Chapter 1, we began to write about Personal Kanban on the Evolving Web blog *http://ourfounder.typepad.com/.* The response was immediate and enthusiastic, especially on Twitter. So we continued to blog, microblog (Tweet), and engage in conversation to test our assumptions with the emerging global Personal Kanban community of practice. This led to a series of Personal Kanban-related consulting engagements and then to the dedicated Personal Kanban website *personalkanban.com.*

We hope to continue the conversation, and welcome you to connect with us and other Personal Kanban practitioners.

FACEBOOK

Join us on Facebook to meet and engage with other
Personal Kanban practitioners. Share your ideas, ask
questions, post your Personal Kanban photos, discuss
your Personal Kanban experiences. Keep apprised of the
latest Personal Kanban-related blog posts, podcasts, pre-
sentations, webinars, and engagements. Simply "Like"
the Personal Kanban Facebook page to become a member
of the PKFlow community.

TWITTER

Follow us on Twitter: @personalkanban, @ourfounder
(Jim), @sprezzatura (Tonianne). More than any other,
it was the Personal Kanban community on Twitter that
truly made this book possible. Active Personal Kanban
practitioners worldwide shared their successes, discussed
their challenges, and exchanged their customizations.
When you tweet about your Personal Kanban experiences, be sure to use the hashtag #PKFlow to ensure other
members of the Personal Kanban community can join the
conversation.

BLOGGING

A quick Google search demonstrates the level of Personal
Kanban engagement on the Web. Around the world,
practitioners are blogging about their innovations and
experiences using Personal Kanban, from managing
home renovations, to prepping for a holiday gathering,
to tracking children's chores or confidence levels. These

types of blog posts have greatly enlivened the Personal Kanban discussion on Facebook and Twitter. We welcome you to share your stories directly with the Personal Kanban community. Be sure to share a link to your Personal Kanban-related blog posts on Twitter (remember to add #PKFlow to your tweets) or on the Personal Kanban Facebook page.

And of course you can read the Personal Kanban blog at personalkanban.com.

LIMIT YOUR WORK-IN-PROGRESS

ACKNOWLEDGEMENTS

We dedicated this book to those individuals who, long after they left us, continue to inspire us each and every day in ways they never could have fathomed. We are likewise grateful for the following people, whose actions and input not only enhanced this book, but enriched us in the process.

For Jim:

Vivian has been there since the start of this Personal Kanban ride and has been vital for its growth. My wife was there at the beginning, providing insight on learning styles, the intricacies of ADHD and Asperger Syndrome, and stages of language development. As a speech pathologist, Personal Kanban's application were immediate and obvious. So, not only has she provided award-winning support by making it possible for us to write this book, she even inspired us to push the ideas forward in the first place. Thank you, Bunchie.

Ann C. Miner was the first to help me find discipline in my writing, and she was back to help make this book tighter. I told myself a long time ago that my first book would acknowledge her first and foremost. She tirelessly worked with me while we were in university and beyond. She has always been a harsh critic and an awesome philosophical sparring partner.

My friend and colleague *Corey Ladas* has been a superlative sounding board, providing the key piece of commentary that truly helped this book evolve. Corey and I spent hours discussing Lean, Agile, motivation, economics, social media, communication, philosophy and much more. His keen and creative mind has been wonderful to be around. And, as the book says, he and I kicked our joint Personal Kanban all around the office for well over a year.

Tonianne DeMaria Barry—a year of work, every day, dreaming, building, growing, and sometimes arguing. One could not ask for a better collaborator.

William Rowden and *David Anderson*—without either of whom there would be no Personal Kanban. William, who in response to a random inter-office email dropped a copy of Kent Beck's *XP Explained* on my desk and started a decade of mutual exploration, software creation, business ownership, first-person-shootering, and process improvement. David, who wrote a book that forced the two of us to discuss Goldratt's Theory of Constraints for over a year and led to the kanban evolution.

Donald and Jennifer Benson—My parents led by example helping shape my love of thinking, disdain for convention, and yearning for fairness. Most importantly, they gave me a sense of always-yet-never questioning belonging to home and country.

Adding fuel to the fire are the regulars at Seattle Lean Coffee: *Jeremy Lightsmith, Garth Tutor, Joe Justice, Wes Maldonado, Jon Bach, Dawn Hemminger*, and *Jesse Brown*.

And my friends and colleagues who, over the years, joined me for a stroll through an idea, provided that key epiphany-producing comment, or thoughtful redirection. They include *Nancy White, Jay Fienberg, John and Susan von Seggern, Jerry Michalski, Howard Rheingold, Jon Ramer, Jeanine Anderson, Greg MacKinnon, Ken Thompson, Frank Provenzano, Ed Vielmetti, Kevin Jahne, Alan Cady, Bart Cima, Chad Nabity, Simon Bone, Christopher J. Zorn, Monte Page, Jessica Margolin* and *Trevor Blake*.

▶ **If you pick one thing to do, and do it completely, people will notice.**
~ Trevor Blake

LIMIT YOUR WORK-IN-PROGRESS

For Tonianne:

Duncan, who through hell, heaven, and all that lies between, has been my guide. My protector. My champion. My Virgil. But with a cookie pocket. An indomitable spirit, he made even the most exhausting parts of the journey bearable. Who knew it would take a Scottish Spaniard to show me the proper way to be Italian. It is for all these reasons and countless others that my appreciation is boundless, my respect infinite, and my love eternal.

Frances DeMaria, who nurtured my curiosity, believed in my voice, and above all taught me the value of critical thinking. Whether they were intentional or by default, her lessons were myriad and far-reaching: Read no less than three sources before drawing a conclusion, *Show, don't tell!* when you write, and never be the smartest person in the room if you ever expect to grow. These are gifts less tangible than possessions but of far greater consequence, and for them—and her—I am grateful.

In a culture that celebrates poorly-behaved reality stars and athletes who've fallen from grace, real heroes are often forsaken. Teachers like *Patty Biedelman* are among the unsung. Indefatigable in her quest to inspire her students, Patty was one of Personal Kanban's earliest adopters and most innovative practitioners. Her classroom experiences informed my own thinking about Personal Kanban as a cognitive tool, while her 3am reminders to limit my WIP (and get some sleep) ensured I practiced what I preached. She is an indispensable friend who is in the truest sense a hero and an inspiration to all whose lives she's touched.

For Jim and Tonianne:

The creative genius at Wayworks, *Chris Banks* and *Lynne Faulk*, who designed the cover and page layout respectively. We are beyond excited with how it looks.

Our friends at MarcusBloom, who provided expert web design at a most crucial time. *Simon Marcus, Jabe Bloom, Matt Moran*, and *Ryan Neuffer* were relentlessly generous with their time and a blast to work with.

Ann Miner who can now share the pain of Jim's random capitalization with Tonianne and provided "buckets of awesomesauce" when we most needed it.

We'd also like to thank *Nancy White, Tom McClusky, Carmen Medina, Ross Mayfield, Sue Thomas, Jerry Michalski, Michael Dalton* and *Mary Alice Haft.* All inspirations in their own right, we are profoundly thankful for their time, input, and graciousness.

This book would never have taken shape without the invaluable feedback we received from the initial, vocal adopters of Personal Kanban. When we floated those first blog posts, the following individuals embraced the idea and were quick to provide a sounding board, rapidly self-organizing into a global Personal Kanban community of practice. They include *Paul Eastabrook, Christopher Beer, Patty Beidleman, Joakim Sunden, Peter Hultgren, Maritza van den Heuvel, Joe Dager, Melanie Haven Gilbert, Janice Linden-Reed (and Morgan!)* and *Derek Huether.*

Finally, we thank Chef Jose Andres and the late Ben Ali for the best fuel and ambience we could have asked for.

ABOUT
JIM BENSON

Jim Benson's path to creating Personal Kanban was winding at best. His 20 years since university have seen him build light rail systems and neighborhoods as an urban planner, enterprise software and web sites for major government agencies as the co-owner of Gray Hill Solutions and, most recently, helping create better working environments for teams of all sizes as a collaborative management consultant with Modus Cooperandi. The common thread throughout his history has been the physical, regulatory, technological, emotional, fiscal and political boundaries of community.

Jim has worked with corporate, government, and not-for-profit organizations of all sizes. He helps clients create sustainable collaborative management systems. He and his company Modus Cooperandi combine Lean principles from manufacturing, Agile methodologies from software design, and the communications revolutions of social media, as process and tool infrastructure. The key to making those tools work, however, is developing a culture that supports them.

No bio of Jim Benson would be complete if it did not talk about food. One simply has to follow either his Twitter stream or his Facebook updates to see that his passion for community and innovation is rivaled only by his love for food. He has traveled the world eating, cooking, and discussing food. Picking his favorite dish is as painful as picking his favorite song. Although if pressed, he might say Cantonese *Siu Yoch* or *Wu Goch* represents the highest evolution of human food. But he's been known to fly to Washington D.C. for a Ben's chili half-smoke.

He is @ourfounder on Twitter.

ABOUT TONIANNE DEMARIA BARRY

Tonianne DeMaria Barry's consulting career spans the fashion industry and government agencies, nonprofit associations and Fortune 100 corporations, start-ups and international development. Her academic training in history lends itself well to management consulting, where she contends that especially in business, the present value of the past is often under-appreciated.

Forever asking *Why* and *How* things happen, she helps her clients uncover, analyze, and interpret their institutional artifacts. Leveraging the stories and values embedded within an organization's culture, she helps individuals use their history to establish priorities, achieve goals, and make informed and innovative decisions. Much like Personal Kanban itself, she wants her clients to acknowledge their past and present context, appreciate the interconnectedness and flow of events, and extract lessons from the patterns which emerge so they can plan better for the future.

She has worked with Jim and Modus Cooperandi on a variety of projects, including recent engagements with the World Bank and the United Nations.

In her spare time, Tonianne can be found exploring the world of single malts, enjoying a Central Park hot dog beneath the Bethesda Fountain, or finding magic in the mundane through the lens of her Nikon.

She is @sprezzatura on Twitter.

ABOUT
MODUS COOPERANDI

Performance through Collaboration: Jim Benson chose this motto after years of working with teams and observing their interactions. When team members are stuck, their peers come to their aid. When they have a good idea, others improve upon it. Through collaboration, effective teams find efficiencies, ultimately increasing throughput, decreasing waste, and significantly improving morale.

Modus Cooperandi sees collaboration as the primary vehicle for group performance. Information sharing, cross training, rapid problem solving, group ownership of tasks, reprioritization, and a strong focus on the completion of quality products are the building blocks of successful teams. We have worked with organizations of all sizes, from individuals to multinational corporations and world governments. The fact is, waste occurs when people stop talking, and Modus works with teams to identify the conversations that need to happen now and in the future.

We recognize the pressures placed on groups to perform, and understand that factors like policies, growth, partnerships, and internal politics directly impact that perfor-

VISUALIZE YOUR WORK

mance. Each team or organization has its own dynamic. Modus helps teams learn to create tools and practices that create collaborative systems, make constraints explicit, reward innovation, and provide meaningful performance metrics.

MORE FROM
MODUS COOPERANDI PRESS

Books:

Scrumban: Esssays on Kanban Systems for Lean Software Development

by Corey Ladas

Available on Amazon, iBooks, and at personalkanban.com

Coming Soon:

Scrumban II: Stories of Continuous Improvement

Kidzban: Personal Kanban for Kids

The latest publications and videos from Modus Cooperandi Press are available at:
http://moduscooperandi.com/

INDEX

VISUALIZE YOUR WORK

VISUALIZE YOUR WORK